RECOGNITION OF BOOK AND WORK

Rev. Walters-Sleyon and The Center for Church and Prison, Inc. are engaged in extraordinary work mending lives, reviving hope, and empowering communities to build a transformative movement to end the racialized system of mass incarceration in the United States - a system that has decimated entire neighborhoods, destroyed families, and profoundly altered the life course of millions, especially Black men.

Michelle Alexander-Author: *The New Jim Crow: Mass Incarceration in the Age of Colorblindness*

Rev. Walters and the Center for Church and Prison are doing some of the most important work in the US today. The prison problem is one that has destroyed millions of lives and is a manifestation of irresponsible capitalism, combined with a malicious disregard for the plight of our man. America has crippled itself for generations to come by incarcerating so many Americans without just cause, and the curse is coming back to haunt us. Rev. Walters and this book are part of the healing process necessary for us to try to become an honest and true democracy. I truly respect the work this man is doing.

Dr. Boyce Watkins: *Your Black World*:

In the growing national movement to bring faith voices front and center in the struggle against mass incarceration, the work of Rev. George Walters and his Center for Church and Prison stands out. Locked Up and Locked Down helps explain why the work in Boston is so powerful: it combines an electric theological awareness with incisive analysis of all the ways in which the American way of incarceration expresses the very worst in this culture--the violence, the racism, the contempt for the poor. This is must read for those of us who want to awaken from our slumber and fully commit ourselves to the civil rights struggle of the 21st century.

Rev. Peter Laarman: *Justice Not Jails*- **Los Angeles**

As our nation struggles with mass incarceration and a failed criminal justice system, we turn to religious leaders for answers. This text fills an important need for religious and philosophical discourse on how our current policies must change to reflect an agenda of restoration and reconciliation and in the best of the Christian tradition, redemption. If humanity is created in the image of God, we must find ways that reflect GOD's ethic of restoration. Rev. George Walters- Sleyon has advanced the conversation.

Dr. Harold Dean Trulear: Howard University School of Theology

Locked Up and Locked Down: Multitude Lingers in Limbo captures the existential angst of mass incarceration in the United States criminal justice system and its debilitating consequences for especially Blacks men, the family, and the Black community. It is not a legal analysis but an existential analysis with the goal towards strategic solution development and intervention. It poignantly defends the claims that mass incarceration in the United States, fueled by the war on drugs, racism, poverty, and the high rates of recidivism is a humanitarian crisis. It is very descriptive, analytical, and prescriptive with a mandate that also calls upon the Church in America to intervene. I highly recommend it to criminal justice reform advocates, religious leaders, students, and especially relatives of incarcerated individuals. My listeners are riveted to their radios every time Rev. Walters appears as a guest. Now they have a book to study, discuss and share with others.

Joe Madison: *The Black Eagle: The Joe Madison Show*

LOCKED UP
AND
LOCKED DOWN:

MULTITUDE LINGERS IN LIMBO
REVISED EDITION

LOCKED UP
AND
LOCKED DOWN:

MULTITUDE LINGERS IN LIMBO
REVISED EDITION

J. George M. Walters-Sleyon

This book was printed in the United States of America.

First Edition published in 2009.

Second Edition Published in 2013

Library of Congress Control Number: 2009901460
ISBN: Hardcover   9781312790797
                  Softcover   9781312791756

To order additional copies of this book, contact:
www.lulu.com
www.georgewalterssleyon.com
www.churchandprison.org
Email: gwalt436@gmail.c

Prayer

I must find my own Judge

I must find a fitting justice

A judge who respects the dignity of me

A justice that rescues from the pain of indignity

I must find my own judge

I must find a fitting justice

(J. George Mitten-Gmah Walters-Sleyon)

Contents

Dedicated to:
My Mama and My Papa
Mama Tanneh "introduced" me to God

Papa Andrew Mitten-Sleyon-Wreh Walters

Introduced me to reading.

Mama and Papa live in heaven.

But your Balluu loves you.

My Mother, My Father,

Bodily absence cannot erase your love.

Distance cannot erase memories.

You love me, and I know it.

I love you and will always do.

Acknowledgments

This book has evolved over the years. It has transformed into a composite of thoughts, reflections, and anecdotes tracing actions of human perversion. It is criminal justice centered yet theological, existential, narrative-oriented, and structured toward the telling of a particular story. It is the story and recurring theme in the United States socio-cultural, socio-legal and socio-religious narrative. It has taken me several years to mature into the knowledge, meaning, and understanding of the story-a difficult story for some and an empowering story for others.

Writing this book would have been impossible without the help of friends, relatives, professors, clergymen and praying mothers. I owe a debt of gratitude to several individuals. I thank my wife for her unflinching support and dedication. Finally, my deepest gratitude to God in the name of Jesus Christ who set me free. Peace to all who read these words and to the multitude of men, women, and children caught in the human machine of the United States penal system.

A special acknowledgment to Dr. Emory L Perkins, LCSW, ACSW, CCDVC, LMFT, Assistant Professor at Bowie State University's Department of Social Work.

Nevertheless here are social problems before us demanding careful study, questions awaiting satisfactory answers. We must study, we must investigate, we must attempt to solve; and the utmost that the world can demand is, not lack of human interest and moral conviction, but rather the heart-quality of fairness, and an earnest desire for the truth despite its possible unpleasantness.
(W. E. B. Du Bois, *The Philadelphia Negro, p. 3).*

J. George M. Walters-Sleyon

Locked Up and Locked Down: Multitude Linkers in Limbo

Foreword

By Rodney L. Petersen, PhD
Executive Director, Boston Theological Institute

Locked Up and Locked Down focuses on one of the most profound anomalies of the twenty-first century that the nation that most trumpets freedom and democracy is also the one with the highest rate of incarceration: one in 100 Americans is in prison or jail at the time of the publication of this book.

Even more scandalous is the racial disparity that accompanies these numbers, that one in nine black men, ages 20 to 34, is behind bars; and for black women, ages 35 to 39, the figure is one in 100, compared with one in 355 for white women in the same age group. This raises the obvious question: why is there such a disparity?

Many experts attribute the increase in America's prison population to tougher sentencing. For example, the famous "three strikes" rule has led to an increase in the time people spend in prison. Then, too, there are the cycles of violence that more overtly accompany economic deprivation and social disadvantage and lead to the a-social behavior dealt with through the criminal justice system.

It is ironic that at just the time that America celebrates a person of African American heritage in the White House, we are drawn in this Study to a continuing racism that shapes the underlying factors behind elevated rates of incarceration.

The historical conditions that compound this racism have social ramifications that perpetuate it, a story that is well told by Orlando Patterson in Rituals of Blood: The Consequences of Slavery in Two American Centuries. Walters-Sleyon picks up the thread and draws us to prison as a rite of passage for many young men and as surrogate welfare for a failed social policy. Drawing upon the insightful work of Christopher Marshall, he shows how all of this is at variance with a guiding biblical vision as well as from the intent in the founding of prisons as places of moral and social rehabilitation.

Writing for church and academy alike, Walters-Sleyon draws us through his own story of imprisonment to conceptions of the dignity and rights that come into play in the courtroom. For example, against a philosophy of the right laid out by G. W. F. Hegel that finds a criminal still to be a criminal even when he has been punished and freed, Walters-Sleyon points to the biblical vision and Augustinian theological tradition for a liberating and restorative understanding of the human person, a view taken up by Pope John Paul II.

While acknowledging that incarceration is appropriate for crime, Walters-Sleyon targets arbitrary arrest, racially motivated sentencing, the criminalization of black men and their commodification by a growing commercial prison industrial complex in a study that easily traverses the worlds of theory and practice. Following the guidance of The Covenant with Black America, Walters-Sleyon concludes with practical steps for churches and civic organizations that are prophetic, rational, critical, and pragmatic.

> *As long as you will not cease devouring and destroying the poor, I shall not cease accusing you of it...Leave my sheep alone. Let my flock be. Do not destroy it, if and if you do, do not complain that I accuse you.*
> (St. John Chrysostom).

Introduction

Today I believe in the possibility of love; that is why I endeavor to trace its imperfections, its perversions.
(Frantz Fanon: *Black Skin, White Mask p. 42).*

The United States admits more inmates than it releases.[1] The US has 5% of the world's population but 25% of the world's incarcerated population. Caught in the US criminal justice system are over 7.5 million individuals under correctional supervision. These figures reflect a steady increase in the rates of mass incarceration based on race, gender, and age since 1972 with a 600% increase by 2008.[2] In 2014, the US had 2.4 million individuals incarcerated with 688,000 released each year and 12 million individuals recycled through local jails. At over 722,000, the jailed population is high because of those waiting to face trial or too poor to post bail with 300,000 jailed for misdemeanor offenses often in one year (Wagner 2015). The American Civil Liberties Union (ACLU) notes:

> Men and women charged with and convicted of crimes are overwhelmingly poor…80-90% of people charged with felonies are found to be indigent by the courts. The majority of those incarcerated lack a high school diploma, have below-average literacy levels, and have few job opportunities. It is not surprising, then that up to 60% of former inmates remain unemployed one year after release from prison. Without adequate education and employment, people often struggle to

---

[1] Steven Raphael and Michael Stoll, *Do Prisons Make Us Safer* (New York, United States, Russell Sage Foundation 2009, 4)
[2] Pew Charitable Trust, State of Recidivism: The Revolving Door of America's Prison (Washington DC, United States, 2011, 5)

pay for even the most basic of necessities – food, shelter, utilities, childcare, and transportation.[3]

According to Michelle Alexander, mass incarceration in the US, "operates as a tightly networked system of laws, policies, customs, and institutions that operate collectively to ensure the subordinate status of a group defined largely by race."[4] Alexander's definition of mass incarceration reflects a trend in the US that disproportionately incarcerates those of a racial and economic background. She refers to this trend as the development of a *racial caste* and *undercaste* system that "denotes a stigmatized racial group locked into an inferior position by law and custom."[5] The ACLU notes that the US has the highest incarceration rate in the world. The country

> Imprisons more people-both per capita and in absolute terms-than any other nation in the world...The current incarceration rate deprives record numbers of individuals of their liberty, disproportionately affects people of color, and has at best a minimal effect on public safety.[6]

Race and poverty drive mass incarceration in the US with a third category of "below-average literacy." The US is severe in punishing offenders, but its severity is racially targeted. Racial particularities drive the severity of punishment in the United States penal system.[7] Those between the ages of 20-35 are the largest population of inmates. The targets of the United States penal system are notably: Blacks, Hispanics, and poor Whites. Thus, the US operates a legal

---

[3] American Civil Liberties Union, *Modern Day Debtor's Prisons: The Way Court Imposed Debt Punish People for Being Poor* (New York, NY, 2014, 3)

[4] Michelle Alexander, *The New Jim Crow: Mass Incarceration in the Age of Colorblindness* (New York, The New Press 2010, 13)

[5] (Alexander, 2010, p. 12)

[6] American Civil Liberties Union, *Banking on Bondage: Private Prisons and Mass Incarceration* (New York, NY, 2011, 5)

[7] (Federal Bureau of Prisons, 2015)

system of mass incarcerating human beings, a disproportionately high number of whom are African Americans.

In Massachusetts, Hispanics are 10.1% of the total population, but 28% of those incarcerated. Blacks are 7.9% of the population but are close to 35% of those incarcerated and detained. Hispanics and Blacks are less than 19% of the total population of Massachusetts but are over 55% of those incarcerated in Massachusetts.[8] The population statistics are based on the 2012 Census Bureau statistics on race.

Massachusetts' rate of racial incarceration reflects a national trend. Blacks and Hispanics are more than 60% of those incarcerated in the United States with Black men consisting of over 42% of those incarcerated in the United States' prison system.

I argue in this book that the element of permanent guilt lies at the heart of the American criminal justice system, especially in relation to minority men, women, and juveniles. Furthermore, I argue that the offender is still a human being, a candidate for redemption, rehabilitation and full reintegration into the society as a viable and contributing citizen.

While we do not condone egregious crimes against other human beings, we can conclude, considering its long-term implications, that mass incarceration is the most powerful form of sociopolitical and economic disempowerment and alienation. The systemic marginalization of offenders from mainstream America reflect the social implications of mass incarceration. The economic consequences include intergenerational impoverishment and the lack of sociopolitical and economic mobility. Also, increase in HIV/AIDS, tuberculosis, mental illnesses and suicide underscore the increasing health implications in the American penal system. Mass incarceration in the United States does not only generate human suffering but budgetary constraints for the state and the federal government. According to the Pew Charitable Trust 2011 Report: *State of Recidivism: The Revolving Door of America's Prisons.*

> Since the early 1970s, prisons have been the weapon of choice in America's fight against crime. Between 1973 and

---

[8] *Massachusetts Department of Correction Prison Population Trends 2012*

2009, the nation's prison population grew by 705 percent, resulting in more than one in 1 in 100 adults behind bars. This growth came at substantial cost, with annual state and federal spending on corrections exploding by 305 percent during the past two decades, to about $52 billion. During that same period, corrections spending doubled as a share of state funding. It now accounts for one of every 14 general fund dollars, and one in every eight state employee's works for a corrections agency.[9]

This book presents an existential analysis of mass incarceration in the United States, a disturbing reality for many, but especially for Black and Hispanic men, women, and juveniles. Blacks are 13% of the United States population but are overwhelmingly over 50% of the American correctional population. According to Alexander, Black men are incarcerated in the United States today than in 1850. Rebecca Thorpe argues that incarceration has become a "revolving door" for Blacks with many under correctional supervision-caught between incarceration and parole or probation in urban America. 75 percent of prisoners imprisoned in the state of New York came from seven predominantly Black and Latino communities in the city of New York in the late 1980s. Also, 25,000 of New York's inmates annually came from poorest neighborhoods, including The Bronx, East New York, Brownsville, and Harlem. Furthermore, 23,000 prisoners were released on parole annually into these same poor communities. According to Thorpe,

Given a statewide recidivism rate of 47 percent, 15,000 of them were shipped back 'upstate' behind bars within the span of one year. While one in three African American and one in six Latino men in their twenties are in prison, one probation, or on parole nationwide, these figures pale in comparison to deindustrialized cities in the Northeast, where approximately two in three

---

[9] The Pew Charitable Trusts 2011 Report: *"State of Recidivism: The Revolving Door of America's Prisons* p. 5.

African American men between the ages of twenty and twenty-nine are under some form of correctional supervision.[10]

I started this research in 2007 out of curiosity as a result of a political philosophy course I was taking at the time. The course was on the German philosopher Georg W. F. Hegel. The main text was Hegel's *Elements of the Philosophy of Right*. On crime and punishment, Hegel is a retributivist who believes in the idea of "once a criminal always a criminal." He does not believe in deterrence nor does he make room for mitigating factors. In his view on crime and punishment is the notion of inherent criminality that perpetually criminalizes the offender even for the most non-violent crime. I became interested in Hegel's views on crime and punishment in light of the high rates of incarceration of Blacks and Hispanics, and the link between mass incarceration and the commercial prison—industrial complex. I was curious about the link between the increase in the prison-industrial complex and the stigmatization of Black men as criminals, the social implications for Black boys, and the Black family structure. While I do not see racism in every punishment meted out for crimes committed by minority men, women, and youths, I argue in this book that there is a need for a cogent investigation into the high rates of incarceration of minority men, women, and children in the United States' penal system. I believe it is unjust for the United States to condone the mass incarceration of human beings mainly for racial and economic gains rather than for crime, punishment, and rehabilitation.

This book also explores the lenses through which Black men are criminalized in the United States. I contend that the offender is not inherently a criminal. Apart from personal responsibilities, this book argues that there are sociopolitical and economic factors informed by the consciousness of the American society that should be considered if one is to understand the offender, his crime, and his criminality.

---

[10] Rebecca U. Thorpe, *Democratic Politics in an Age of Mass Incarceration* in *Democratic Theory and Mass Incarceration* (Oxford University Press, 2016, p. 21) (Loic Wacquant, *Deadly Symbiosis: When Ghetto and Prison Meet and Mesh* (SAGE publication, Vol. 3(1) London, 2001) cit. Thorpe

A prescriptive goal for this book is to appeal to civic and religious organizations to intervene in ways that will dismantle mass incarceration in the United States. For example by:

- **First**: Investigating the war on drugs, the link between mass incarceration and prison as an industrial enterprise, the transformation of sentencing laws, e.g., maximum sentences, Three-strikes laws, life without parole, especially for non-violent crimes.
- **Second**: Educational campaigns with an emphasis on education and training as preventive measures on the front-end. This process should engage religious and civic organizations, local re-entry organizations/after-prison-care providers, family support groups, etc.
- **Third**: Allowing former prisoners to have access to housing and employment is fundamental to reducing the high rates of recidivism. Direct intervention strategies with an emphasis on rehabilitation are essential pathways to encouraging economic mobility for former prisoners and their families.

The book is both academic and personal. However, it does not explore the details of academic technicalities at length. This is especially true of the section on Hegel. References to major figures are made to underscore their existential connections to the overall narrative. The goal is to emphasize the portions of their works that convey their identity with human suffering and alienation. In that light, this book presents an existential analysis of over 7.4 million individuals in the United States' criminal justice system. According to Dr. Martin Luther King, Jr.

> Many of the ugly pages of American history have been obscured and forgotten. A society is always eager to cover misdeeds with a cloak of forgetfulness, but no society can fully repress as ugly past when the ravages persist into the present.[11]

---

[11] King, 1968, p. 109

Structurally, this book is descriptive, analytical and prescriptive. I have divided it into three subsections.

Section 1 is descriptive. Chapters 1, 2, 3, and 4 provide a descriptive analysis of the high rates of incarceration and detention in the United States' criminal justice system. It identifies the conditions and structures upon which mass imprisonment strives in the United States. This section concludes by highlighting the need for prison reform and strategic intervention as a result of the high rates of recidivism and other collateral consequences.

Chapters 6 and 7 of Section 2 argue that mass incarceration is inhumane and devalues human beings. An offender is a person of inherent worth and dignity. To reduce the offender to a category of inherent criminality as the American criminal justice system perpetuates is unjust. Crime is not "infinite," and the offender is not an inherent criminal. To criminalize the humanity of the offender is to prevent the possibilities for rehabilitation, restoration, and reintegration. This section explores the works of St. Augustine, W. E. B. Du Bois, Pope John Paul II, and others. It argues for an understanding of the offender beyond the use of racial stereotypes as lenses through which crimes are punished. Also, it concludes with an analysis of the role of the Black Church and the need for strategic intervention from religious, civic and humanitarian organizations.

The third section is prescriptive. Chapter 8 concludes with suggestions that call for strategic intervention proactively. It focuses on four fundamental responses: *Prophetic, Rational, Critical* and *Pragmatic.* These responses are means of intervention in the high rates of incarceration and recidivism in the United States' prison system.[12] This book is also an account of my lived experience.

My Story

It is said that no one truly knows a nation until one has been inside its jails. A nation should not be judged by how it treats its highest citizens, but its lowest ones.
(Nelson Mandela).

The United States of America operates a gulag. It is called mass incarceration. The world has ignored the scale of human incarceration in the United States, its consequences, and racial particularity. I stumbled upon the presence of this American gulag as a result of a philosophical curiosity. Nevertheless, a curiosity that providentially brought me to the first-hand experience of mass incarceration in the United States and its painful reality.

It was five o'clock in the morning on March 27, 2008, when a friend dropped me off at the Greyhound bus station in Syracuse, New York. I was on my way to Toledo University in Ohio to attend a conference, scheduled for March 28-29, as a presenter and a guest singer. We said good-bye, and he drove my car back to the house.

I had been invited to present a paper on *Post-war Reconstruction and Ethical Imagination*. With much anticipation, I looked forward to the upcoming moment of intellectual exchange at the conference. It was also the highlight at the time of my academic training as a first-year Doctor of Theology (Th.D.) student.

At 6:30 a.m., I boarded the Greyhound bus. It was scheduled to make a quick stop in Rochester, New York before moving on to Buffalo where I needed to change buses to Cleveland and finally to Columbus, Ohio, my final stop.

Between Syracuse and Buffalo, I decided to take a quick nap but woke up just before we reached Rochester for our stop. We arrived in Rochester at around 8:30 a.m. Some people got off the bus, and others came on. Just before we could continue, two border patrol officers got on board and asked to see our identification cards. One came directly over to me, sat beside me, and asked to see my identification card. I gave him my Massachusetts driver's license and my student identification card. He went to the back of the bus to inspect them.

After inspecting my cards, he returned and sat next to me again. This time, he said his records indicated that I had traveled to Canada in 2005 and to Mexico in 2007 respectively and that he was going to arrest me. Before I could respond, he interrupted and said that I had overstayed my student visa. Again, before I could tell him that I had never traveled out of the United States since 1999, that I was not on a student visa, and was a student at Boston University, he interrupted and ordered me off the bus. I informed him that I was a clergyman and on my way to attend a conference at the University of Toledo in Ohio where I was scheduled to speak. He interrupted me and to my dismay, shame, and humiliation, as everyone on the bus listened and stared at me, I was taken off the bus and arrested. Hastily, they returned my Greyhound ticket and took my luggage off the bus. In utter dismay, I was transported to the patrol office in Rochester. While in the patrol car, I told him I have never traveled to Canada or Mexico and explained my status. He heard me but said nothing. With my mind racing, I processed my abysmal condition.

As we entered the patrol office in Rochester, I noticed an assortment of over a hundred suitcases and bags bundled in a heap in the corner. At the office, they processed me and set a bond on me. As I sat there wondering what was going to happen next, the officer told me to call any friend or relative to come and collect my bags. He was taking me to the Federal Detention Facility, and if no one came to get my bags after two weeks, they would add them to the assortment of bags and suitcases I had noticed upon entering the building prepared for trashing. I shuddered at the thought of my bags trashed, and at the thought of the rest of the suitcases and bags in their different shapes and colors trashed. I frantically tried to think of someone who could travel to Rochester and collect them. One of the bags had my CDs, and the other, my suits purchased on a tight student budget. I could not bear the thought of losing them. I called everyone I knew to tell them what was happening to me and where I was. I had no idea what was awaiting me.

As I sat in the office, I saw the border patrol officers bring in more people arrested on the Greyhound buses and Amtrak trains. They were all Black men, except for a Jamaican woman with two kids. She was pregnant, and her kids were crying. The officer got irritated by the noise and put them behind bars while he interrogated the mother. She was crying at this moment as the children kept screaming for their parents. She said she was not undocumented. Her husband had her documents, but fright and shock prevented her from providing the right information. I saw a fellow with a video camera taping the interrogation, and at the time, I assumed he was from an organization that had some legal rights to record the arrest and the interrogation. The officers were uncomfortable with his presence. The officer processed the pregnant woman and the men with their bags and suitcase taken from them. I began to wonder: If the officers trashed the bags and suitcases, what about the valuables in them? Are they simply trashed, or are they opened individually, searched, priced items extracted, and the rest trashed? Who takes the priced items out of the bags? Is someone searching these bags and suitcases, and selling them to the public? Is someone making money off the bags of these people? Unfortunately, those released after two weeks do not get their bags and suitcases returned to them. The prison officers transport them to the nearest bus station, and if no one picks them up, they are on their own.

I also began to think about the fares of those taken off the Greyhound buses and Amtrak train like myself. What becomes of their money? One would think their ticket fares would be returned to them immediately for the rest of the journey. Unfortunately, their tickets are returned to them, but not the fares. After the arrest, the border patrol officer transports the arrestee to the border patrol office. There they are processed and usually, a bond of $10,000, set for their release. They are then whisked off to the Federal Detention Facility or County Jail if the FDF is full. How will their fares be reimbursed? I do not know, but one thing is certain: They are placed in detention or jail and deported after seeing a judge or must linger between indefinite detention and indefinite deportation. Like the ambiguity surrounding their bags and suitcases left at the border

10

patrol office when they were arrested, their ticket fares remain with Greyhound Bus and Amtrak. I could not stop pondering these things. But for now, I told myself I must concentrate on my problem and stop this mental wondering.

Thinking about my arrest in the patrol office, I repeated my claim to the officer who arrested me. I told him that I have never traveled out of the United States at the time. Furthermore, that I was not illegal nor on a student visa or with an expired visa. I had a legal status. But to my utter dismay and with a smile on his face, he responded, "It wasn't you; it was someone else; forget it." I waited for him to say, "Get your bags and let me take you back to the bus stop." But to no avail, I only heard, "forget it." "Forget it?" I repeated in my mind. I asked him if I could be released. He said no. I could not believe what I was hearing. I was speechless. I pondered the phrase, its implications, consequences, and impacts on my life: "Forget it"—he was saying, he lied to arrest me. How many people did he lie on to arrest I wondered? "Forget it." Did he care that he was shattering my life, my dreams, my hopes, and my aspirations or that I could languish in jail if no one came to my rescue? But he knew they could detain me indefinitely without knowledge about my deportation. If it wasn't me, why was he so quick to arrest me? Why didn't he listen to me? Did he have to arrest me to make up his quota for the day? I shuddered at the flippancy with which they regarded my humanity; my destiny tossed; my dreams consigned to the wind; and my expectations for the day, the weekend, and my life trampled upon as insignificant. I wondered how many people, especially Blacks and Hispanics, he must have harmed by lying on them and telling them to "forget it" while consigning their lives to destitution and despair. I trembled within with fear and anxiety. If I am guilty, I must admit my fault, but if I am not guilty, why not listen to me? Even the guilty ought to be heard. I was arrested at 8:45 a.m. and held behind bars at the patrol border office. At 3:00 p.m., I was whisked off to the Federal Detention Facility in Batavia/New York. In less than twenty-four hours, I found myself frantically trying to establish contact with the outside world as freedom evaded me and fright consumed me.

11

At the front desk in the detention facility, they processed me and took everything from me including my book. While they were processing me, my phone rang, and I noticed it was a friend calling to inquire. As I tried to pick it up, the officer screamed at me. He said he was going to break the phone if I touched it. I watched as it rang and went off. I fought back the tears as they watched me. After the processing, I was stripped and given a blue suit together with two pairs of underwear, socks, and a pair of slippers, sheets, and toiletries. They assigned me a deportation officer and confiscated my cell phone and other belongings. The only personal belongings I kept were my Bible and my glasses. After that, they assigned me to a unit and bed. It was after 8:00 p.m. I was exhausted, and sleep could not allow me to stay awake.

I woke up at 6: am the next morning, and I didn't want to open my eyes, hoping this nightmare would dissipate. I knew where I was. I was tangibly in detention and was not having a dream. Depressed and frustrated, I began to pray and ask God what was happening. It was then that I heard a still small voice saying to me, "Remember you have been working on this; look around you and see." It was surreal, but it was real.

In the spring of 2007, I had taken a political philosophy course. The main text was *Element of the Philosophy of Rights* by the German philosopher Georg Hegel. What stood out for me in the reading and what set me off on a personal research journey was Hegel's position on crime and punishment. In simple terms, Hegel is a retributivist. He believes in the idea of once a criminal always a criminal. Hegel does not take into consideration external factors that could be socio-political, economic, psychological or existential in deciding a case. Considering the little I knew about mass incarceration at the time, Hegel's argument that once a criminal always a criminal set me off on a personal research journey in the spring of 2007. By the end of the summer of 2007, I had a manuscript of about 300 pages, hoping to debunk Hegel's claims. I submitted the manuscript to my professors. Unfortunately, it was rejected based on the claim that it had no human touch. I after that put it down and decided to focus on my studies.

In prison the next morning, I eventually opened my eyes. A part of me wanted to deny it, but my surrounding reminded me. The bunk bed that I was sleeping on, the blanket, the blue suits that had become my identity, the slippers, the black-and-white sneakers, the tiny toothbrush that refused to clean the middle and end of your mouth, not forgetting the eyes that gaze at you. Something within me said, "You are in lock-up; get used to it." But I knew I could not get used to it because it was not my end, I assured myself.

At breakfast, I got to see all the other detainees in my unit. I noticed a higher number of Black men from Africa and the Caribbean than Latinos, Caucasians, or Arabs. I became curious. I wanted to hear their stories. I began to initiate some friendship. I sat at a table with three other detainees. We introduced ourselves since I was the newest one there. I told them that I was originally from Liberia, and I was brought in the day before. One was an elderly gentleman. I also noticed he was eating a different diet from the one they served the rest of us. He introduced himself and said he was from Nigeria. He had a special diet because he had diabetes. The fellow on my right was from Guinea. He was a musician. He was arrested in Rochester during the '07 Christmas holidays on his way to a program and family gathering. The fellow on my left was from Mali. He was the youngest and was looking very depressed. As the days dragged on, he ate less and less of his food. There was another fellow from another African country; four of us were from West Africa. We became friends. I later realized that my unit was not the only one filled with Africans or those from the Caribbean.

There were two major halls for immigrants; most of the occupants were Black men. I met some of them on the second day in the yard. There were older and younger men from every corner of Africa and the Caribbean. They wore blue suits and brown jackets like us. They spoke English very well. Through several conversations, I got to know that many of them had acquired secondary and postsecondary education before coming to the United States. They regretted their present state and felt their lives wasting away. Incarceration targeting Black men had not been a part of their expectations of the United States—if only they had remained in

13

Africa or the Caribbean they said. But the saddest part about their arrest was that most of their relatives in Africa and the United States had little or no clue as to what had happened to them. Some of them were arrested off Greyhound buses or Amtrak trains and by now, had little contact with their relatives and friends. They had depleted the little money they possessed when arrested. Their families in Africa only knew that they were in the United States; as to their present condition, most families were unaware. It was then that I also began to understand why most families in Africa with relatives in the United States and other parts of Europe sometimes complain that they don't hear from them, and some even assume their relatives have died or abandoned them.

I noticed one morning the man from Guinea was very depressed. I asked what was wrong, and he said nothing, but I knew he was depressed since he had no definite knowledge about his case. He was thinking about his future, and as a young man, he knew his life was wasting away. He had a bond of $10.000, and he didn't know how to raise it. His future was bleak. He didn't know his deportation date, even though he had asked for voluntary deportation. I encouraged him and told him not to give up. I saw his eyes wet with tears, but he quickly dried them. I wondered, what would happen to him if he does not pay his bond or deportation does not take place very soon. But he was not the only one in this situation.

On the second day of my detention, I also noticed everyone going to their bunk beds late in the afternoon. The others went to the bathroom, which provided scant privacy. Anyone in the dining room, which was a few feet from the beds, could see who was in the bathroom. I was afraid of going in there. But at 4:00 p.m., I discovered it was lockdown time. Lockdown is when every activity involving the detainees is brought to a standstill until everyone is counted per their photos and cleared. Lockdown included restricting every detainee to their bed. Every movement ceases, and except the officers on duty. During lockdown, the correctional officer looks into your face to determine whether the face he is looking at matches the picture he has in his hand.

14

Before the day could end, someone invited me to a prayer meeting that took place at 8:00 p.m. At the prayer meeting, I met other detainees. One of the facilitators was a detainee from Angola. He was very young, maybe in his early twenties, but very passionate about God and the Bible. He must have had a true conversion experience before his arrest because he appeared more than a prison convert. There were also Nigerians, Latinos, a fellow from Sri Lanka, and others from the Caribbean. To my surprise, the preacher was the older gentleman from Nigeria I had met during breakfast. He was ordained in the eighties and was serving a church in the United States. He had been in the United States for a long time. His wife and three kids were American citizens, but he was not. One would think because of the status of his wife, he would automatically gain his legality and walk out, but that was not the case. When I met him, he had been in detention for the past five months. He was previously in a county jail where they mixed him with hardened criminals and those convicted of a felony, an experience he characterized as one of the most degrading because he was not a criminal or charged with a felony. He had filed his case on several occasions and could only await his fate. But for now, he did what he knew best: preach the gospel of Jesus Christ and bring hope to those who came to listen. When I asked him what he missed most because of his detention, he responded, "My freedom."

Seated in the corner during the meeting was a very sad and petite man. But his words and mannerism betrayed his sophistication and education. I decided to find the time to converse with him. The moment came, a perplexing one indeed. He was a prominent Ghanaian journalist who was at one time selected as one of two African journalists to attend a conference in the United States. He had written several articles and had worked with prominent organizations in Ghana and the United States. At the time of his arrest, he was a student specializing in international politics. They arrested him on his way from Massachusetts to Alabama and placed a bond of $10.000 on him. When we met, he had been in detention for six months. He depleted the funds he had, and without money, it was difficult to contact his relatives. He was frustrated and had no money. As we spoke, I saw tears well up in his eyes, and I wanted to cry with him. By the end of my third day in detention, I had heard bits and pieces of stories about the length of time several of the detainees had spent in the facility. The maximum was about six years in this facility with many still in "limbo."

The word limbo implies ambiguity. It is a Catholic doctrine which connotes a place situated between hell and heaven—a place of uncertainty for the dead, especially babies. The Catholic Church no longer holds to this doctrine because the logical necessity cannot be justified. The detainee to be deported is not certain of his fate since he awaits the decision of the judge, which may take a while in coming. Sometimes, because of the lack of a breakthrough in his case, his uncertainty as to when they will deport him or his inability to pay the bond of $10,000, the detainee might ask to be voluntarily deported. But like many of the men who asked to be deported voluntarily; voluntary deportation was not or is not a quick fix. Thus, the detainee is frustrated and depressed. He does not know when they will deport him; he does not know whether he will be released, and since the bond is too high for his family to pay, he must painfully endure the ambiguity and uncertainty of his situation while wetting his pillow with tears in the middle of the night. With a $10,000 bond on his head, his fate is unpredictable. Furthermore, with no relative or friend of means around to shoulder the bond, the detainee is kept in limbo. He finds himself in this stalemate with his life wasting away. In most cases, the African has no relative around. Unlike the Mexican who has the border to cross, the African has the Atlantic Ocean between his current state and where he originated.

A typical day in detention includes breakfast, lunch, and supper. Supper was either at 4:00 p.m. or 5:00 p.m. with breakfast the next day at five, six, or seven, depending on the specific detention facility. Because of the time lapse between supper and breakfast, one automatically learns the tricks of not eating their entire ration but preserving some for the long night. The rest of the time goes to sleeping, conversing, or gazing dejectedly at the surrounding walls that have come to define one's fate.

On the fifth day in the morning, I was sitting in a secluded corner of the room when they supplied clean sheets and towels. Because I was not familiar with the various announcements, I missed the supply of clean sheets. I went to the officer on duty for some, but to my dismay, he said his boss had told him not to provide me with clean sheets or towels. I went to my bunk bed; it had no sheet on it, the green mattress in its harshness gazed at me. I simply sat on it and refused to lie on it. I picked up my Bible and started to read. It was the only book I could take with me. I read the poetic books of Job, Ecclesiastes, Song of Songs, and was reading the book of Isaiah when this incident occurred. I turned to Isaiah 7 and found strength in verse 9: "If you do not stand firm in your faith, you will not stand at all." I had this experience on the 1st of April 2008.

There is danger in accepting your detention and incarceration as an act of fate. The danger is for one to stop pushing for release through legal means no matter how impossible it may seem. To relax and accept the situation is to subject oneself to personal defeat. Especially if you believe in your innocence, there is no reason why you should accept the situation as your inevitable fate. I saw a young man in his late twenties, laughing, joking, and annoying others as though walking in total freedom. He had a job in the kitchen for which he was proud and walked arrogantly. I heard he had been in there for a while, and it seemed he had accepted his condition as his destiny. For some, a moment of relaxation and ease is a moment of deep reflection and empowerment, a time to refill their quest and longing to be free. For others, it signals a moment of "settling down," of arriving at the point of escape from the pressures of the outside world. In this context, the free food, a false sense of security, the medical attention, the absence of bills to pay for some reflects a state of stability.

At 3:00 p.m. on Tuesday, the first of April, the officers announced my release. The New England Annual Conference of the United Methodist Church had posted my bond, and I was told to pack whatever supplies they had given to me in the pillowcase and proceed to the front desk for final processing. Standing at the desk in the hall, one of the fellows I met during breakfast came over to

17

say good-bye. In that short time, we had become friends. He had been in detention for over five months and did not know what his fate was. A bond of $10,000 was placed on him before I came, and he did know how he was going to raise that amount. He asked the judge to deport him voluntarily but had not heard from the judge. I encouraged him to be strong and to keep on praying. Later he came over to say good-bye. Standing there, I told him I was going to keep praying for him and that he should never give up. Meanwhile, standing behind us was the officer on duty. He interrupted the conversation and said: "I will not release him." I turned around and jokingly asked, "Why?" The officer's response was shocking and delivered with sincerity. He said, "If I release him, I will not have a job." I was speechless. He saw the shock in my eyes, and I saw the rage in his eyes as his face turned red. Immediately another officer came to collect me to take me to the main desk for processing. I have concluded that was a providential interruption. I knew he had seen the shock on my face, and he knew I saw his wrath swelling in his face as it turned red, but I had escaped a verbal exchange that might have jeopardized my release. I was whisked off, and in less than thirty minutes, I took off the brown jacket, the blue suit, and the black-and-white sneakers and returned the beddings. I was back on the outside in the world with the suddenness with which I entered detention. They tossed me out just like they tossed me in.

The conversation with the officer haunted me. It was the precise confession to the use of human bodies as means of economic gain, job creation and profit in the American penal system. The practice is particularly one that reflects the historical use of Black Bodies in the United States and the scars it has left on the souls of several generations. According to Dr. Martin Luther King Jr.,

> For years the Negro has been taught that he is nobody, that his color is a sign of his biological depravity, that his being has been stamped with an indelible imprint of inferiority, that his whole history has been soiled with the filth of worthlessness. All too few people realize how slavery and racial segregation have scarred the soul and wounded the

18

spirit of the black man. The whole dirty business of slavery was based on the premise that the Negro was a thing to be used, not a person to be respected.[13]

Did he realize the implications of his statement? The young man that came to see me off was a classic example of thousands of people arrested and facing deportation but not knowing when deportation might take place. In their frustration, like him, they have requested for voluntary deportation but still have not been deported. Some with the usual bond of $10,000 have languished in detention for months to years and still detained; only existing in limbo because of the ambiguity surrounding their detention.[14]

---

[13] Martin Luther King, Jr., *Where Do We Go from Here: Chaos or Community* (Beacon Press, Boston 1968) p. 38.

[14] The criminal basis of the detainees is unclear. According to the Human Rights Watch 2007 report on the National Statistics on the Deportation for Crimes, there exists an ambiguity with respect to the reason for deportation. Only recently has the Immigration and Customs Enforcement (ICE) agency within the Department of Homeland Security provided statistics on criminal convictions warranting deportation from the United States. According to the Human Rights Watch, "For reasons that are unclear, in its regular press updates the agency always touts its deportation of violent criminals, but keeps vague the other categories of immigrants deported...In one press statement, announcing the deportation of 562 "criminals aliens,' ICE chose to highlight presumably three deportees who were removed for 'Aggravated assault,' 'drug trafficking,' and 'lewd and lascivious acts on a child.'" It concludes by quoting a special observation from an immigration analysis unit from Syracuse University that declares, "Despite the interest in aggravated felonies, very little is currently known about how often aggravated felony provisions are in fact used. The government publishes no statistics on the number of individuals it has sought to deport, or actually deported, on aggravated felony grounds. A literature search has not turned up any other sources with relevant statistics." www.hrw.org/reports/2007/us0707/6.htm Accessed: 23/06/2009

> *In his eyes, I am despised*
> *In his sight, I am despised*
> *In his eyes, I should linger not*
> *In his sight, I should languish*
> *Despised and not-to-be-seen I must know*
> *Disappear and assert not I must acknowledge*
> *Who am I but a warning?*
> *Who am I but a warrant?*
> *A warning he knows not*
> *A warrant he sees not*
> *Since in his eyes, I am not*
> (George Walters-Sleyon)

For the officer, because he must have a "job," detainees must be available. His daily bread depends on the arrest and detention of "illegal immigrants," many of whom are of African descent as reflected in the total population in US jails and prisons. The logic is that a certain number of detainees must be kept in the facility to maintain the momentum of detention and deportation in the public's eye. Since a certain number of detainees must be detained to keep the facility operating, a certain number of arrests must be done to maintain the quota. In this case, it seems justice and security are not the main reason, but business, a certain number of detainees must be kept and a certain amount released to balance the quota. The $10,000 reflects the price to have people lingering between actual deportation and indefinite detention. Someone might say, they should have known better not to have entered this country illegally or overstayed their visa. I met several gentlemen from Africa who requested for voluntary deportation but have been detained for more than six months. While in detention, their belongings were trashed. They are guilty of entering the country illegally or overstaying their visas. However, the question remains, how long will they linger between indefinite detention and indefinite deportation?

Prisons and detention camps are for profit. The targets are economically disadvantaged individuals- poor Whites, Latinos, and

Blacks. The criminalization of Black men and youths, the sequestering of the Black adult male and female as co-conspirators to deviancy, racial influences in the sentencing process, harsher and punitive sentences like three-strikes-you-are-out, and the high rates of racial profiling. The impacts of mass incarceration and the industrialization of prisons are real and debilitating.

In the End, we will remember not the words of our enemies, but the Silence of our friends.
(Martin Luther King, Jr.).

Mass incarceration in the United States reflects the fundamental means by which systemic racism plays itself out. This book acknowledges the individual causes as well but largely interprets them within a broader historical, sociopolitical, and economic framework.

After reflecting on my situation, I have come to see both detention and deportation, especially for the Black immigrant and the domestic incarceration of Black men, as influenced and informed not mainly by the crime they have committed. Instead, their detention and incarceration are fundamentally informed and influenced by their skin color, the racialization of their humanity and the criminalization of who they are. The Black man or women directly from Africa or the Caribbean or other places in the Diaspora have a higher chance of being deported than any other race or nationality. Also, the African American has a higher chance of being arrested and incarcerated in America than members of other ethnic groups. The Black male immigrant is criminalized just as much as the Black male who is a citizen. Both are Black men of African descent, subject to arbitrary arrest, racial profiling, and racial forms of criminalization, racially motivated sentences, incarceration, detention, and deportation.

It is in this light that I analyze the high rates of detention and incarceration of Blacks in the United States. I will be looking at its disproportionality, social consequences, and existential implications. I prefer to use "Blacks" instead of Africans,

21

Caribbean, or African Americans. The differences in terms are not as relevant as one might believe when looking at the prevailing statistics on the number of Black people detained for deportation and incarcerated in the United States criminal justice system. The Black man is known as a person of African descent or ancestry. While the use of the term, "people of African descent" and "Black men" or "Black women" may raise some questions for the White African, I want to suggest that there isn't a difference of complexion between the White African in America or Europe from the White American or European. The White African escapes the experience of being African or Black African simply because he or she is White. Being a person of African descent in Europe and the United States denotes different interpretations and experiences for the Black African or African American and the White African. As previously indicated, this book is not designed to be an academic text but an informative text providing a narrative of mass incarceration and its implications in the United States. As such, the style is to highlight the main points after each major section or chapter for the sake of clarity.

Main points:
- Immigrants and prisoners sustain detention and prison facilities across the United States.
- The United States prison system is fundamentally an industrial enterprise with little focus on rehabilitation for prisoners.
- Africans, Black Caribbean, and African Americans are considered "Black" in the United States criminal justice system with little or no distinction.
  - "Blackness" is the "color of crime" in the United States' social conscience and criminal justice system.

It was not then a question of crime but rather of color that settled a man's conviction on almost any charge. Thus Negroes came to look upon courts as instruments of injustice and oppression, and upon those convicted in them as martyrs and victims.
(W. E. B. Du Bois, *The Relations of Negroes to Whites in the South*).

A DESCRIPTIVE DISCUSSION

CHAPTER ONE:
G. W. F. Hegel: Once a Criminal always a Criminal.

The United States has by far the world's highest incarceration rate. With 5% of the world's population, our country now houses nearly 25% of the world's reported prisoners. We currently incarcerate 756 inmates per 100,000 residents, a rate nearly five times the average worldwide of 158 for every 100,000. In addition, more than 5 million people who recently left jail remain under 'correctional supervision,' which includes parole, probation, and other community sanctions. All told, about one in every 31 adults in the United States is in prison, in jail, or on supervised release . . . Either we are home to the most evil people on earth or we are doing something different . . .

Senator Jim Webb, *What's Wrong with Our Prisons?*
Boston Sunday Globe-Parade, p.4

Hegel's *Elements of the Philosophy of Right* reflects a systematic development of the concept of "right" as it develops into an "idea of right." It is a part of his entire philosophical system. Interestingly, while Hegel's *Philosophy of Right* is highly conceptual and theoretical, one cannot help but notice the influence of his theory on the formulation of policies regarding the sentencing of criminals in the 21st century.

Hegel's views on crime and punishment have been interpreted as retributivist, semi-retributivist, or a non-retributivist. I was interested in two dominant claims in his theory about the criminal in the *Philosophy of Right*: (1) that the offender is still considered a criminal after their time in prison, and (2) that the offender is still a criminal even at the granting of pardon from the sovereign. Hegel argues that by committing a crime, the offender has lost his rights. Only God can effectively pardon a criminal in the realm of the spirit, but in the concrete world of sociopolitical and economic activities, the criminal will remain a criminal and will always be viewed a criminal as legislated by the state.

Hegel believes the state is "supreme." Based on this notion, the primary victim of any crime in the state is the state itself, not the individual victim. Furthermore, the state has the power to disenfranchise the offender by rendering him or her a "rightless citizen," thus stripping them of their rights as citizens. Crime is the transfer of rights to the state. Per Hegel's argument, a pardon is the remission of punishment, but it is not a cancellation of rights (the right to meet crime with a crime). On the contrary, the right of the states continues to apply, and the pardoned individual remains a criminal. Clemency does not mean he or she has not committed a crime. Religion may cancel *Aufhebung* punishment and criminality but what has been done can only be undone in the spirit by the spirit itself. In so far as it is accomplished in this world, it is to be found only in the majesty [of the sovereign] and is the prerogative of the sovereign's ungrounded decision.[15] Per the above, the criminal will always be a criminal even after his or her punishment. To better understand Hegel's argument in this context, one must understand his notion of "right" about crime and punishment.

---

[15] G. W. F. Hegel, *Elements of the Philosophy of Right* (Ed. Allen Wood, Cambridge University, 1991), PR. 282, (see: PR. 97A, 99) for *Aufhebung* Hegel in English implies "Sublation." It means to "preserve", to maintain and also to "cause to cease" i.e. to "put to an end" (See: The Science of Logic, pp. 45, 46, 107).

Hegel claims what he calls "abstract right"[16] for everyone, but with a condition. Abstract right indicates one's inherent claim to individual right manifested through the will of the individual in the world.[17] Right is first an abstract entity and secondly, a concrete entity. A right implies the will of the individual to himself as purely a subjective person. Since every individual has the abstract right, which also becomes concrete in the world, Hegel claims every individual must exist according to his commandment of right, i.e., "Be a person and respect others as persons."[18] On the other hand, that right can be taken away when a person commits a criminal act because for Hegel, "crime in itself is an infinite injury."[19] Crime is an infinite injury that affects the state as the supreme entity. It is for this reason that the criminal will be perpetually stigmatized as a criminal even when he has paid the due penalty for his crime. The criminal is still a citizen but a citizen with no right recognized by the state.

In this model, crime is both physical and spiritual. It implies that the criminal is first an inherent criminal and secondly, a concrete criminal. For Hegel, the sovereign can only pardon the criminal based on his punishment in the world but cannot restore their right nor decriminalize their humanity.[20]

Hegel argues that crime reflects the will of the offender; therefore, any punishment incompatible with the crime committed

---

16 Ibid., PR, 2, 19.

17 Ibid. PR. 4.

18 Ibid., PR. 36.

19 Ibid., PR. 218, "Crime in itself is an infinite injury, but as an existence [*Dasein*], it must be measured in terms of qualitative and quantitative differences and since its existence is essentially determined as a representation [*Vorstellung*] and consciousness of the validity of the laws, its danger to civil society is a determination of its magnitude, or even one of its qualitative determinations."

20 Ibid., PR. 100: According to Hegel: "The injury [*Verletzung*] which is inflicted on the criminal is not only just in itself (and since it is just, it is at the same time his will as it is in itself, an existence [*Dasein*] of his freedom, his right); it is also a right for the criminal himself, that is, a right posited in his existent will, in his action. For it is implicit in his action, as that of a rational being, that it is universal in character, and that by performing it, he has set up a law which he has recognized for himself in his action, and under which he may therefore be subsumed as under his right."

reflects the dishonoring of the criminal. "The action of the criminal involves not only the concept of crime [but] its rationality in and for itself which the state must enforce with or without the consent of the individual's [*der Einzelnen*] volition."[21] Since the crime involved reflects the will of the criminal, and the crime committed is an embodiment of his consent to be punished. His consent is no longer needed when he stands before the judge because of his crime, which expresses his will, takes away any recognition of his abstract right, will, or freedom in the concrete world. Per Hegel, the criminal is "honored" if the state does not consult concerning his punishment since he has already committed a crime that is the expression of his will and right. Hegel argues, "That the punishment which this entails is seen as embodying the criminal's own right," therefore, he is honored. But he is dishonored "if the concept and criterion of his punishment are not based on his act, and he is also denied his right if he is regarded simply as a harmful animal which must be rendered harmless, or punished with a view to deterring or reforming him."[22] Punishment is not a deterrent; it is not restorative, rehabilitative, or transformative. For Hegel, crime is a legal transfer of ones' right to the state. Therefore, punishment, i.e., imprisonment is a necessary measure to implement the taking away of the right of the criminal, and criminalization is the means to enforce the taking away of such right. For Hegel, "The criminal gives his consent by his very act" to be punished. Hegel does not support "reforming" the criminal. Reforming the criminal to prevent future crime is not an issue of priority in Hegel's analysis of crime and punishment.[23]

Thus, the criminal will always be a criminal. Based on the above, only God can pardon a criminal in the realm of the spirit, but

---

[21] Ibid., PR. 100,
[22] Ibid., PR. 100,
[23] Ibid., PR. 100, 101. "Both the nature of the crime and the criminal's own will require that the infringement for which he is responsible should be cancelled [*aufgehoben*] . . . The cancellation [*Aufheben*] of crime is retribution in so far as the latter, by its concept, is an infringement of an infringement, and in so far as crime, by its existence [*Dasein*], has a determinate qualitative and quantitative magnitude, so that its negation, as existent, also has a determinate magnitude."

in this concrete world of human activities, the criminal must be viewed as a criminal and "right-less" in the society even when pardoned by the sovereign of the state. [24]

In summary, it is not difficult to see how Hegel's notion of crime and punishment might be detrimental. It legitimizes a perpetual criminalization of the criminal. The criminal is a citizen, but unlike other citizens, he is right-less. Hegel's theory of crime and punishment are problematic. They contribute to a consciousness of "criminalization" rather than advance cogent solutions towards "decriminalization." This conclusion is especially important within the context of the history of slavery, racism, and discrimination that have informed the development of the American criminal justice system.

It was in detention that I discovered another missing link in my research: the relationship between the high rates of detention of African and Caribbean immigrants for deportation in detention facilities and the high rate of incarcerated African American men across the United States.

As an existential analysis, I want to capture in words the anguish, agony, and despair associated with mass incarceration in the United States' criminal justice system. Mass incarceration engenders feelings of self-negation and distortion. I believe beneath the crucibles of political, economic, and social stability rest the realities of despair, dismay, and desperation for survival. In its harsh reality, the economically and socially marginalized, the detained, incarcerated, and abandoned scream for help and, in their anguish, are forced to question their very existence, their sense of being, and their humanity. [25] This book argues that the offender is a human

---

[24] Ibid., PR. 101, pg. 128 "Yet the concept itself must always contain the basic principle, even for the particular instance. This determination of the concept, however, is precisely that necessary connection [which dictates] that crime, as the will which is null and void in itself, accordingly contains within itself its own nullification, and this appears in the form of punishment."

[25] Ben Campbell Johnson, *Rethinking Evangelism: a Theological Approach* (Philadelphia, The Westminster Press, 1987) 32 "Where did I come from? (Sense of origin), Who am I? (Sense of identity), What is wrong with me? (Sense of alienation), Why am I here? (Sense of meaning) and Where am I going? (Sense of destiny)."

being, a candidate for redemption. I do not believe that the offender is inherently a criminal. What would Hegel say about the enormous influence of racial preference in the sentencing process, punishment as an industrial enterprise? How will Hegel's system respond to historical assumptions and consciousness that criminalizes one group of people? How will he respond to what has now become a multi-billion-dollar industry: the prison-industrial complex in the United States fundamentally fed more by race, poverty, illiteracy, and less by "crime"?

Main points from Hegel:

- Once a criminal always a criminal.
- Hegel is a retributivist; he does not believe in deterrence.
- The criminal cannot be rehabilitated, restored or redeemed.
- The criminal offends the state because the state is supreme.
- The criminal is a citizen but a right-less citizen.
- The humanity of the criminal is criminalized.

Consequences:

- The offender is socio-politically and economically marginalized.
- The offender is prohibited from accessing public and government benefits.
- The offender easily recidivates after release and repeats the perpetual cycle of crime, incarceration, release, and recidivism.

CHAPTER TWO
The Principles of the Four 'Rs'

The criminal is recognized to have rights as a human being, even when he has violated his obligation to society.
(Reinhold Niebuhr: *An Interpretation of Christian Ethics*[26]).

Hegel's argument fundamentally rejects what I refer to as the principles of the four "Rs": Respect for human dignity, Reform in the Sentencing Process, Rehabilitation of former prisoners, and Restoration of former prisoners into the community. These principles are not absolute but provide a platform for discussion and engagement towards strategic solution development.

Respect for Human Dignity

The offender is a human being regardless of his or her crime. Crime does not undermine or relegate the humanity of the offender to second-class human status. Crime is not a determiner of human dignity and worth. If the criminal justice system undermines human dignity, it undermines the sacred thrust of justice. The offender remains a human being. The recognition of their humanity in the criminal justice system provides a means to effective forms of rehabilitation and restoration.

Four historic factors in the American social consciousness militate against the recognition of the inherent dignity of individuals

---

[26] *From Christ to the World: Introductory Readings in Christian Ethics*, Eds. Wayne G. Boulton, Thomas D. Kennedy, Allen Verhey (Grand Rapids, Michigan, William B. Eerdmans Publishing Company,1994) pp. 244.

in the criminal justice system. I explored in various sections of this book:

The racialization of human beings:

The color of the skin as the immediate premise for executing justice in the sentencing process. According to Dr. King, the American social consciousness is influenced by historical race-based treatments. He explains that:

> Racism is a philosophy based on a contempt for life. It is the arrogant assertion that one race is the center of value and object of devotion, before which other races must kneel in submission. It is the absurd dogma that one race is responsible for all the progress of history and alone can assure the progress of the future. Racism is total estrangement. It separates not only bodies, but minds and spirits. Inevitably it descends to inflicting spiritual or physical homicide upon the out-group.[27]

King goes on to define racism as a "tenacious evil" that is, however, "not immutable."[28] The irony of racism he argues is the dilemma it poses for poor Whites who on the one hand have to confront the contradiction between White supremacist ideas and their economic plight. He notes: "White supremacy can feed their egos but not their stomachs. They will not go hungry or forego the affluent society to remain racially ascendant."[29] Finally, King asserts that the fundamental factor in the perpetuation of racism is its inherent goal of "economic exploitation."[30]

---

[27] King, 1968, p. 70.
[28] King, 1968, p. 152.
[29] King, 1968, p. 152.
[30] King, 1968, p. 172.

The rejection of inherent criminality:

It refers to the influence of sociopolitical stereotypes and racial consciousness informed by public policies and legislation as the first reason for sentencing and punishment. The offender is not an inherent criminal.

The dehumanization of the offender:

The ultimate perpetuation of systemic policies in the correctional process to reduce the offender to an object of lesser human dignity and worth. It is influenced by race, prejudices, greed, and insecurity in the American penal system.

The commodification of the offender:

It refers to the reduction of the offender to a commercial product for cheap labor, one that contradicts the concept of humane punishment. Offenders are used as bargaining chips in the exchange process among prison owners, prison investors, wardens, and superintendents. As commercial products to sustain the prison-industrial-complex and promote prison expansion, prisoners are products for job creation for prison workers, guards, and economic revitalization of rural/suburban towns where they construct most prisons across the United States.

Mass incarceration begins by strategically criminalizing the other to justify their incarceration. Cultural criminalization is the process of stigmatizing the other from advancing in the sociopolitical and economic structures of the society. Mass incarceration in the United States depends on the practice of historical racial criminalization of Blacks.

Criminalizing the "other" distorts the sacredness of human dignity. To criminalize the other is to stigmatize the other as evil, ugly, an object of extreme restriction, use, and abuse.

Religion claims that every human being is created with the "Spark of the Divine." For Christianity and Judaism, the Book of Genesis declares in Chapter 1:26:

And God said, let us make man in our image, after our likeness.

9

In the Quran, Allah is intimately involved with the creation of humanity:

> *Verily We created man from a product of wet earth; then placed him as a drop (of seed) in a safe lodging; then We fashioned the drop into a clot, then We fashioned the clot into a little lump, then We fashioned the little lump into bones, then clothed the bones with flesh, and then produced it another creation. So, blessed be Allāh, the Best of Creators! [23:12-14].*

Similarly, Hinduism depicts the creation of human beings as children of *Dharma*. In the *Siva Purana*, Brahma said:

> *Dharma, the means for achievement of everything, born of me, assumed the form of Manu at my bidding. I created from the different parts of my body innumerable sons. I was then prompted by Siva present within me and hence I split myself into two, one had the form of a woman and the other half that of a man. That man was Svayambhuva Manu, the greatest of the means of creation. The woman was Satarupa, a yogini, an ascetic woman. Together they created beings. Their sons and progeny are spread over the world both mobile and immobile.*

These religious traditions believe in the 'sacred' of the person. One may either interpret the above quotations as a collection of meaningless religious platitudes or seriously analyze the contradictions between them and the tolerance for the high rates of incarceration of human beings in the United States. With over 7.2 million individuals caught in the criminal justice system, the issue of mass incarceration in the United States has reached a pivotal stage that demands humanitarian, religious, and international attention.

Statistics on race in the Federal Bureau of Prisons from 26 September 2015 reflect disproportionate rates of racial incarceration in the US prison system (Federal Bureau of Prisons 2015).

Race	# of Inmates	% of Inmates
Asian	3,138	1.5%
Black	77,455	37.7%
Native American	3,938	1.9%
White	120,977	58.9%

In the early 20th century, prominent American sociologist W. E. B. Du Bois analyzed the American criminal justice system as an institution founded on the principles of racial superiority. Its goal, he argues, was to re-enslave free Blacks considering the huge economic downturn White businesses suffered after the Emancipation Proclamation. Furthermore, Du Bois argues that the increase in the Black prison population was consistent with an increase in racialized forms of incarceration. He concluded that the American criminal justice system focused mainly on the "color of the crime."[31]

With the focus on the color of the crime, a form of racial criminalization emerged in the sentencing process. According to the Sentencing Project 2016 report: *The Color of Justice: Racial and Ethnic Disparity in State Prisons*; "African Americans are incarcerated in state prisons at a rate that is 5.1 times the imprisonment of whites. In five states (Iowa, Minnesota, New Jersey, Vermont, and Wisconsin), the disparity is more than 10 to 1." Furthermore, "In twelve states, more than half of the prison population is black: Alabama, Delaware, Georgia, Illinois, Louisiana, Maryland, Michigan, Mississippi, New Jersey, North Carolina, South Carolina, and Virginia. Maryland, whose prison population is 72% African American, tops the nation. In eleven

---

[31] Zuckerman, 2004.

states, at least 1 in 20 adult black males is in prison." Also, "In Oklahoma, the state with the highest overall black incarceration rate, 1 in 15 black males ages 18 and older is in prison. States exhibit substantial variation in the range of racial disparity, from a black/white ratio of 12.2:1 in New Jersey to 2.4:1 in Hawaii." Similarly, "Latinos are imprisoned at a rate that is 1.4 times the rate of whites. Hispanic/white ethnic disparities are particularly high in states such as Massachusetts (4.3:1), Connecticut (3.9:1), Pennsylvania (3.3:1), and New York (3.1:1)."[32]

Harsher sentences also fueled the development of mass incarceration. For example, three-strikes and mandatory sentences became common and disproportionately imposed. Three-strike is the sentencing policy that two prior convictions with a third conviction will earn you the maximum sentence for the crime, which in the case of the war on drugs or other sentencing policies is twenty-five years or life behind bars for most states. The Sentencing Project notes:

> Policies that impose harsher penalties based on criminal history will have a disproportionate effect on African Americans. In California, for example, blacks constitute 29% of the population, but are 44.7% of the persons serving a 'three strikes' sentence, according to the California Department of Corrections, Second and Third Strikers in the Institution Population, Sacramento, CA: Data Analysis Unit. (February 2004). These disparities take on added significance due to the extreme disparities created by such policies. A non-violent offense in California that might otherwise lead to no more than a few years in prison becomes a sentence of 25 years to life when treated as a third strike offense.[33]

The organizing factors of mass incarceration include the "War-on-Drugs" -three-strikes sentencing policies, the decline in parole eligibility and the institution of other punitive measures to

---

[32] The Sentencing Project, *The Color of Justice: Racial and Ethnic Disparity in States Prisons*, p. 3.
[33] www.Sentencingproject.org/rd_brownvboard[1].pdf 4,

encourage longer prison time. The American criminal justice system does not prioritize rehabilitation.

Reform in the Sentencing Process

A criminal justice system is a mirror in which a whole society can see the darker outlines of its face. Our ideas of justice and evil take on visible form in it. Thus we see ourselves in deep relief. Step through this looking glass to view the American criminal justice system and ultimately the whole society it reflects-forms a radically different angle of vision.
(Jeffrey H. Reiman, *The Rich Get Richer and the Poor Get Prison: Ideology, Class, and Criminal Justice).*

Mass incarceration and its state of dehumanization signal a need for reform. Such a reform requires justice rather the influence of external factors particularly in light of the extraordinary number of individuals imprisoned.

According to Michelle Alexander, the United States' criminal justice system is breeding a "caste system" of individuals perpetually marginalized from the sociopolitical and economic life of America because of their conviction records. Without a cogent investigation and reformulation of sentencing laws and policies, more people will end up going to jail and prisons especially for nonviolent offenses. A major factor increasing the prison population is the role of persecutors. She writes:

> Most prosecutors' offices lack any manual or guidebook advising prosecutors how to make discretionary decisions. Even the American Bar Association's standards of practice for prosecutors are purely aspirational; no prosecutor is required to follow the standards or even consider

them...Armstrong learned the hard way that the Supreme Court has little interest in ensuring that prosecutors exercise their extraordinary discretion in a manner that is fair and nondiscriminatory.

Armstrong's lawyers found it puzzling that no white crack offender had been charged, given that most crack offenders are white. They suspected that whites were being diverted by federal prosecutors to the state system, where the penalties for crack offenses were far less severe. The only way to prove this, though, would be to gain access to the prosecutors' records and find out just how many white defendants were transferred to the state system and why. Armstrong's lawyers thus filed a motion asking the district court for discovery of the prosecutor's file to support their claim of selective prosecution under the Fourteenth Amendment.[34]

Race, racism, and poverty are major organizing factors related to mass incarceration. They serve as important lenses for prosecutors. One cannot overemphasize the need for objectivity beyond race in the American criminal justice system. Also, the exploitation of crime, punishment, and discipline is a blight on the United States' criminal justice system. To exploit crime and punishment as means of economic revitalization and job creation undermine the principles of justice.

---

[34] (Alexander, 2010, pp. 112-113) "If sentencing were the only stage of the criminal justice process in which racial biases were allowed to flourish, it would be a tragedy of gargantuan proportion. Thousands of people have had years of their lives wasted in prison-years they would have been free if they had been white. Some, like McCleskey, have been killed because of the influence of race in the death penalty. Sentencing, however, is not the end, but just the beginning. As we shall see, the legal rules governing prosecutions, like those that govern sentencing decisions, maximize rather than minimize racial bias in the drug war. The Supreme Court has gone to great lengths to ensure that prosecutors are free to exercise their discretion in any manner they choose, and it has closed the courthouse doors to climes of racial bias."

Rehabilitation leads to Adequate Reintegration in the Society

More individuals are experiencing re-incarceration due to socio-economic and health challenges in their post-prison lives. Post-prison challenges are some of the most difficult moments of recovery for formerly incarcerated individuals. The stigma of incarceration and the impacts of a felony record are major hindrances to employment and socio reintegration, especially for Blacks. According to the Pew Center on States 2011 report:

> 45.4 percent of people released from prison in 1999 and 43.3 percent of those sent home in 2004 were reincarcerated within three years, either for committing a new crime or for violating conditions governing their release... The new figures suggest that despite the massive increase in corrections spending, in many states there has been little improvement in the performance of corrections systems. If more than four out of 10 adult American offenders still return to prison within three years of their release, the system designed to deter them from continued criminal behavior clearly is falling short. That is an unhappy reality, not just for offenders, but for the safety of American communities.[35]

Before the 1970s, rehabilitation was the goal in the American correctional system. The shift began when privatization, mass incarceration, and profiteering became the mantra of punishment. Rehabilitation is no longer a major priority in the criminal justice system since it reduces profit and jobs.[36]

---

[35] The Pew Center on the States: *State of Recidivism: The Revolving Door of America's Prisons*, p. 2.

[36] Shichor, David, *Punishment for Profit: Private Prisons/Public Concerns* (London, Sage Publications, 1995) "When a private company is contracted for the management of a prison; the employees are directly responsible to the private corporation and its executives. The employees receive their instructions from private executives, and ultimately their paycheck comes from the private company; they are hired, fired, promoted, demoted, rewarded, and disciplined by the management of the private company...Thus, by the delegation of legitimate power to the corporation, the government loses direct control over

The development of strategic programs for inmates to facilitate adequate reintegration has become secondary. Emphasis on rehabilitation includes the development of pre and post-release programs with the focus on education, skills development and other forms of employment-ready programs.

Reduction in the high rates of recidivism depends on the economic survival of the former prisoner. When accompanied by laws, public policies and economic incentives, emphasis on programs designed for holistic reintegration deter recidivism and reoffending. Furthermore, the parole system is successful when combined with the board of probation in some respect and not seen as continuous punishment. It demonstrates the fact that the pre-sentence reports are available to the parole board to enable them to make adequate decisions based on a chronological sequence of events in the life of the inmate. The inmate can be considered for probation or parole and not kept behind bars with thousands of dollars spent on them. A comprehensive understanding of what leads to the failure of parole or probation on a regular basis is worth investigating to avoid the repetition of failure as the rates of individuals under correctional supervision continues to increase.

Restoration

Injustice anywhere is a threat to justice everywhere. We are caught in an inescapable network of mutuality, tied in a single garment of destiny. Whatever affects one directly, affects all indirectly.
(Martin Luther King, Jr).

Restoration hinges on the principles of just care. It is justice that is fair, judicious and transparent. This form of justice pursues the wellbeing of individuals who have broken the law and are

---

the correctional staff who deal with inmates punished by the criminal justice system that represents society." P, 57.

required to make restitution through punishment. But they must be ultimately restored as viable members of the community.

In 2002, the United Nations Economic and Social Council passed a resolution requesting all member states to "draw" on resolution named: *Basic Principles on the Use of Restorative Justice Programs in Criminal Matters* response to punishment in the penal systems of member states and the need to prevent crime and recidivism. An important aspect of the resolution is for member states to recognize the need to use alternative means of conflict resolution that will lead to community security by including the offended and community in the process.

> Restorative justice is an approach to problem solving that, in its various forms, involves the victim, the offender, their social networks, justice agencies and the community. Restorative justice programmes are based on the fundamental principle that criminal behaviour not only violates the law, but also injures victims and the community. Any efforts to address the consequences of criminal behaviour should, where possible, involve the offender as well as these injured parties, while also providing help and support that the victim and offender require[37]

That justice will militate against the full inclusion of the individual who has violated its principles is alien to the inherent principles of justice. In that light, justice cannot help but be restorative. Justice based on the retributive justice system is highly punitive. Justice as distributive emphasizes the healing nature of justice, while justice as restorative deals with the holistic reintegration of the offender into the society as a repentant and restored member.

---

[37] United Nations Office on Drugs and Crime: *Handbook on Restorative Justice Programmes*, p. 6.

CHAPTER THREE
The "Situation."

Our victims know us by their scars and their chains, and it is this that makes their evidence irrefutable. It is enough that they show us what we have made of them for us to realize what we have made of ourselves.

(Jean-Paul Sartre: *The Wretched of the Earth*).

A ccording to the Pew Charitable Trust, one in every one hundred persons in America was behind bars in 2008.[38] The International Centre for Prison Studies wrote in 2010 that the United States incarcerates 748 inmates per 100,000. The Pew reports, "…for some groups, the incarceration numbers are especially startling. While one in 30 men between the ages of 20 and 34 is behind bars, for Black males in that age group the figure is one in nine."[39] White men age 18 or older were one in 106; Hispanic men age 18 or older were one in 36; Black men ages 18 or older were one in 15, and Black men especially age 20-34 were one in 9.[40] In 2011, the lifetime likelihood of imprisonment for all women was 1 in 56, White women: 1 in 111,

---

[38] www.pewcenteronthestates.org: "One in 100: Behind Bars in America 2008," 5. "The United States incarcerates more than any country in the world, including the far more populous nation of China. At the start of the New Year, the American penal system held more than 2.3 million adults. China was second, with 1.5 million people behind bars, and Russia was a distant third with 890,000 inmates, according to the latest available figures. Beyond the sheer number of inmates, America also is the global leader in the rate at which it incarcerates its citizenry, outpacing nations like South Africa and Iran. In Germany, ninety-three people are in prison for every one hundred thousand adults and children. In the United States, the rate is roughly eight times that, or 750 per 100,000." 5

[39] Ibid., 3: "One in 100: Behind Bars in America 2008."

[40] Ibid., 6, "One in 100: Behind Bars in America 2008." 6.

Latina women: 1 in 45 and Black women: 1 in 18. Lifetime likelihood of imprisonment for all men: 1 in 9, White men: 1 in 17, Black men: 1 in 3, Latino men: 1 in 6.[41] Writing on the topic: *Racial Impact Statement as a Means of Reducing Unwarranted Sentencing Disparities*, Marc Mauer of the Sentencing Project argues that:

> By the early 21st century, the scale of incarceration for African Americans had reached dramatic proportions. Projections by the Department of Justice show that if current trends continue, a black male born today has a one in three (32.2%) chance of spending time in state or federal prison in his lifetime. Comparable figures for Latino males are one in six (17.2%) and, for white males, one in seventeen (5.9%).[42]

Mauer states the causes for the high rates of incarceration for Black men. Among the many socioeconomic and legal factors, he highlights the following: "Disproportionate crime rates, disparities in criminal justice processing, the overlap of race and class effects" and finally "impact of 'race-neutral' policies."[43]

This chapter presents an analysis of what I call the 'Situation.' The situation in this context is the problem that avails itself for an existential analysis. It provides the necessity to interpret life as an incarcerated minority person, its existential and social implications. Thus, the need for strategic intervention.

According to Terry Tempest Williams in *The Covenant with Black America*, the need for us to take an introspective account of our activities given the sociopolitical and economic standing of Black people in America today cannot be overstated. We cannot ignore the urgency to assess our actions concerning the future for the present generation and the need to transcend the trivialization of the present socio-political and economic conditions. She writes, "The eyes of the future are looking back at us, and they are praying

---

[41] Sentencingproject.com: Trends_in_Corrections_Fact_sheet 1980-2011

[42] Marc Mauer, *Racial Impact Statements as a Means of Reducing Unwarranted Sentencing Disparities*, rd_racialimpactstatements.pdf, 22, accessed 01/31/09.

[43] Ibid., 23.

for us to see beyond our own time."[44] *The Covenant* does not mince words in presenting a descriptive analysis of the situation. It highlights the socioeconomic issues that affect every Black person in America. Marian Wright Edelman tries to capture this dilemma in *The Covenant,* by arguing that:

> An unleveled playing field from birth contributes to many poor black children getting pulled into a cradle-to-prison-to-death pipeline that we must dismantle. Imprisonment is the new slavery for the black community. On average, states spend over three times as much per prisoner as per public school pupil.[45]

James Bell describes the process leading to incarceration for Black men as the "cradle-to-prison superhighway."[46] He defines it as a "network of legislation, policy, practice, and structural racism that has fostered the incarceration of Blacks at uncontrollable levels at increasingly younger ages for increasingly minor acts."[47] The warehousing of Black males as a rehabilitative measure has proven not to achieve the intended result. On the contrary, incarceration has turned out to be a booming business. The impact of the cradle-to-prison superhighway is evident in the breakdown of the Black family structure.[48] It was a crime in 1835 to teach a slave how to read. In 1991, two-thirds of those incarcerated were high school dropouts. In the absence of quality education and expectations, low teaching expectations and accountability, lack resource for educational empowerment, the consequences are daunting.

For James Bell, "to reestablish integrity and fairness in the juvenile court system requires an emphasis on reducing racial

---

44 Tavis Smiley, *The Covenant with Black America* (Chicago, Third World Press, 2006), Introductory page.
45 *(The Covenant with Black America,* 2006, p. xiii)
46 *(The Covenant with Black America,* 2006, p. 49)
47 (The *Covenant* with Black America, 2006, p. 49)
48 (Marc Mauer and Ryan Scott King, *"School and Prisons: 50 Years After Brown v. Board of Education,"* http: www.sentencingproject.org/pdfs/brownboard.pdf, the Sentencing Project.")

disparities . . . We must use our collective voice to give voice to the voiceless."[49] Bell sees the increased incarceration of Black men and boys as a problem inherently established by the justice system, its historical perception, and treatment of Black men and boys. Human Rights Watch 2001 report indicates that,

> The prison population of the United States is largely male: as is true around the world, men make up more than 90 percent of all prisoners. Also, in comparison with people outside prison, the inmate population is heavily weighted toward ethnic and racial minorities, particularly African Americans. Overall, African Americans make up some 44 percent of the prisoner population, while whites constitute 40 percent, Hispanics 15 percent, with other minorities making up the remaining 1 to 2 percent. Relative to their proportions in the U.S. population as a whole, black males are more than twice as likely to be incarcerated as Hispanic males and seven times as likely as whites.[50]

Persons-In-Community
Not
Prisons-In-Community

Dr. Walter G. Muelder echoes a similar sentiment.[51] He was Dean of Boston University School of Theology and served as professor of social ethics for twenty-seven years. Dr. Martin Luther King Jr. was one of his students. Muelder refers to the American penal system as an institution of "vengeful penology. . . aided and abetted by the recent growth of the commercial prison—industrial complex which has become a big $140 billion piece of the American economy."[52]

---

[49] *(The Covenant with Black America, 2006, pp. 51-52)*

[50] http://www.hrw.org/reports/2001/prison/report.html.

[51] J. Philip Wogaman (Ed), *Communitarian Ethics: Later Writings of Walter G. Muelder*, (Maine: The Preachers' Aid Society of New England in cooperation with BW press, 2007) xi.

[52] (Wogaman, 2007, p. 20)

As a Personalist, he asserts the inherent dignity all of human beings. Muelder argued for justice defined within the context of "persons-in-community."[53] Persons-in-community is Muelder's argument for a working solution that recognizes the "poor and disinherited" in the formulation of policies and the implementation of justice. It is in this light that Muelder expresses his frustration at the sentencing process and the high rates of incarceration and detention of minorities. He writes:

> What is the present situation in our prisons and jails? Three-fourths of our new inmates are African-Americans or Hispanics. Color-lining in arrests and sentencing is rampant. One-third of America's young African-American males are now in prison, on parole, or on probation. We have underdeveloped preventive institutions and after-care ministries. The two million persons in jail or prison are four times what it was 20 years ago. . . There is no clear relationship of cause and effect except of a trend in the 'Get tough' movement that advocates harsher sentences, mandatory minimum sentencing laws, bigger and fewer human prisons, minimal rehabilitation programs, decline in Parole, militancy in the drug laws, the failing war on drugs, Three-strikes-and-you're-out laws. About 3,500 Americans (Disproportionately African-American) sit on death row.[54]

For Muelder and others who are disturbed by the sentencing process in the American justice system, one possible option is reforming the sentencing process by adopting practices of restorative justice: "A restorative philosophy based on the ethical perspective that all people, including offenders and victims alike, are and should be treated as persons-in-community."[55] But while racial justice concerning other civil rights concerns has historically been the most talked about issue for the Civil Rights Movement, contemporarily, Africans and people of African descent from the

---

[53] (Wogaman, 2007, p. 20)
[54] (Wogaman, 2007, p. 20)
[55] (Wogaman, 2007, p. 18)

23

Caribbean are also increasingly arrested, detained for deportation, and are receiving little attention. Tamara kil Ja Kim Nopper writes,

> To put it simply, Black immigrants have higher numbers of deportations than Asian, Middle Eastern or White immigrants. For example, in 2002, there were 8, 921 total deportations of Black immigrants, whereas there were only 3, 090 total deportations for Whites and 4, 317 total deportations for Asians and Middle Easterners. Overall, this trend is consistent from 1993-2002.[56]

The Deportation of Black Men

The arrest and detention of Black immigrants have not received the level of attention that other nationalities from Guatemala, El Salvador, Mexico, Honduras, etc., have received. Strangely enough, Nopper argues, "Black immigrants tend to have higher numbers of deportation than Asians and Whites, even though the rate of immigration from Africa and the Caribbean tends to be slower than the rate of Asian and Brown immigrants."[57]

Similarly, Black immigrants had the highest rate of deportation for "criminal" activities compared to "non-criminal" activities between the period of 1993 and 2002.[58] As intimated, the distinction

---

[56] Tamara Kil Ja Kim Nopper; *Black Immigrants are deported in Higher Number than Asians and Middle Eastern Immigrants: Reconsidering Immigrants Rights' Challenge to 'Racial Justice' Work.* www.nathanielturner.com:

[57] Tamara Kil Ja Kim Nopper Ibid.,

[58] Tamara Kil Ja Kim Nopper: "Given the limited attention given to Black immigrants in the immigrant rights discourse, there is of course little mention of the fact that between 1993 and 2002, Black immigrants tend to be deported more for criminal deportations than non-criminal deportations. Asians (including Middle Eastern and many "Muslim" nationalities), however, tended to be overwhelmingly deported for non-criminal deportations than criminal deportations. Between 1993 and 2002, the proportion of criminal deportations out of all Asian deportations ranged between 24-34%, reaching the peak of 34% in 1999. Compare that to the proportion of criminal deportations out of all Black deportations. During 1993 and 2002, criminal deportations of Black immigrants ranged between 57-75%,

between what constitutes "criminal activities" and "non-criminal activities" warranting deportation is still ambiguous.[59] A high rate of criminal deportation is drug-related. In the "war on drugs," minority communities across America are major targets. Unfortunately, as the above report suggests, immigrants from South Asia and the Middle East have gained more sympathy with less deportation than people of African descent. Immediate causes are largely related to race, racism, and poverty. These associations are made regardless of the absence of criminal offense or record. Millions of Americans associate Black men with crime and criminality. The notion that the Black man is a criminal before he breaks the law is inherently problematic. [60]It highlights an historical perception in the process of social stratification. Criminalizing the Black man is done consciously and unconsciously. It is part of the social consciousness regarding Blacks in America. The Black man is viewed suspiciously in the American society.[61] This suspicion is often regardless of his academic, professional, and economic attainment. The existential and psychological implications are enormous.[62] It is in this context that one should seek to understand the Black man behind bars, not as an African American or an African immigrant, but as a Black man largely criminalized, racialized and incarcerated in addition to his or her violent or

---

reaching the peak of 75% in 1996. In short, criminal deportations are more common for Black immigrants whereas the reverse is true for Asian immigrants."

[59] Tamara Kil Ja Kim Nopper., "Generally, criminal deportations mean that you were convicted of a crime, with the result that you are removed from the country after you serve your prison sentence. Any non-naturalized immigrant, regardless of status, can be forcibly removed from the US if they are convicted of an aggravated felony, which is any crime that carries a one-year or more sentence. Non-criminal deportations are usually deportations of immigrants who attempted to enter the US illegally or who overstayed their initial visa without adjusting their status."

[60] Ibid.,

[61] Ibid.,

[62] Ibid.,

nonviolent offense.[63] Mass incarceration is a phenomenon that the American Church cannot ignore.[64]

Main points:

- Black immigrants are deported in large numbers.
- Fewer Blacks than other groups are coming to the United States, but Blacks are disproportionally deported from the United States.
- The distinction between "criminal" and "non-criminal" activities is ambiguous in the immigration system.

The American Church and Racism:

The greatest blasphemy of the whole ugly process was that the white man ended up making God his partner in the exploitation of the Negro. What greater heresy has religion known? Ethical Christianity vanished and the moral nerve of religion was atrophied. This terrible distortion sullied the essential nature of Christianity.
(Martin Luther King, Jr. *Where Do We Go from Here? p. 75).*

Maya Harris begins her analysis with the following questions: "How did we get here? And, given the current trend, can we change direction?"[69] Harris' questions are very important. They should be directed to the American Church. America's racial consciousness and ambivalence towards Blacks' existence started in the American

---

[63] Ibid.,
[64] Ibid.,

[69] (The *Covenant* with Black America, 2006)

Church.[70] Mass Black incarceration in America is not a strange phenomenon to the American Church. The Church in America religiously and historically provided the foundation for the sociopolitical and economic consciousness regarding people of African descent in the United States. Harris's question calls for a lot of "looking within" or "soul searching."[71]

Reform in the sentencing process, the dismantling of mass incarceration and the prison industrial complex can only materialize when the Church of America and its spiritual and secular leaders stand up and declare: enough is enough.[72] According to Rodney L. Petersen, the influencing factors are race, racism, and various forms of racialization as socio-cultural residues of the institution of slavery in the United States.

He argues that racism has permeated the various aspects of America's political and religious life because of its birth through the Church. For Petersen, the "issues of race" have "shaped civil politics and church polity . . . from the fifteenth century to the present . . . The destructive effects of racism in America are well documented from the quays of Charleston to the auction blocks of Anacostia and the banks of Boston."[73] Petersen is a minister. He advocates for restorative justice as an alternative to the retributive justice system. According to Petersen, "In fact, one author [James Q. Whitman] has recently argued that our political system and the impact of slavery upon American society have helped to define the treatment meted out to those who have broken the law and are deemed criminals."[74]

---

[70] Ibid.,

[71] Ibid.,

[72] Gayraud S Wilmore, *Black Religion and Black Radicalism: An Interpretation of the Religious History of Afro-American People* (New York: Orbis Books, 1994).

[73] Robert W. Pazmino, and Rodney L. Petersen, Eds. *Antioch Agenda*, (New Delhi: Indian Society for the Promotion of Christian Knowledge, 2007), 261, 263 He writes, "American culture has been shaped by the politics of race. We may not like this. We may try to deny this. We may not move beyond this even though the social and personal ills attributable to slavery have long been documented."

[74] Ibid., 264 (Whitman connects America's view of crime with the "leveling down" of our political system and with the impact of slavery upon American society such that the

He goes on to argue that racism and the privileges derived from it have informed the way America has defined people of African descent. For him:

> Racism, discriminatory behavior or prejudice towards those of another race, has been defined in terms of its ideological, structural and historic significance for the stratification of population in order to promote or maintain privilege. Race, along with socioeconomic status, ethnicity, gender, religion and other factors shapes how a person views the world.[75]

Per Petersen and Harris, salient factors have influenced the penal policies and practices of mass incarceration in the United States. They include historical racism in the justice system, the police's perception of Black men, racial profiling, the tendencies to suspect and arrest Black men, the activities of the prison industrial complex and the criminalization of Black men.[76] Unfortunately, based on the absence of objectivity, the media portrays Black men as "super-predators."[77] As a result, every Black man is criminalized in the eyes of the public and viewed with skepticism and suspicion regardless of his identity or origin. Criminalization of Black men

---

treatment meted out to criminals parallels that given to slavers. —See Whitman, James Q. *Criminals Punishment and the Widening Gap Between America and Europe* [New York: Oxford University Press, 2003]

[75] Ibid., 263.

[76] U.S. Sentencing Commission, *"Special Report to Congress: Cocaine and Federal Sentencing Policy"* (February 1995)-http://www.ussc.gov/crack/execsum.pdf ("the 1991 Household Survey shows that 52 percent of those reporting crack use in the past year, as opposed to distribution, were white"); The Sentencing Project, "Crack Cocaine Sentencing Policy: Unjustified and Unreasonable, "available at http://www.sentencingproject.org //pdfs/1003. pdf (approximately 2/3 of crack users are white or Hispanic").

[77] *(The Covenant with Black America, 2006, p. 7)* In his book: *Body Count: Moral Poverty . . . And How to Win America's War Against Crime and Drugs* (New York: Simon& Schust, 1996) that Dilulio co-wrote with William Bennett and John Walters, Dilulio suggests that "a late 1990s juvenile-crime explosion will be driven by a rising tide of . . . deeply troubled young men." He had earlier "attracted uncritical attention from the left and the right for his talk of the growth of a 'super-predator' caste of feral young males born of the absence civil society, families, and churches in many parts of America." Excerpted from *"The Real John Dilulio"* by Eli Lehrer of The Heritage Foundation, February 7, 2001, archived at http://www.heritage.org

serves as a prism regardless of its distortion or limitation. It is the claim that Blacks commit more crime than Whites, Hispanics, or any other nationality; therefore, they must be criminals in addition to the media's role as facilitators of such stereotype. It perpetuates a negative cultural stereotype and imagination about Blacks in America. For W. E. B. Du Bois,

> Negroes came to look upon courts as instruments of injustice and oppression, and upon those convicted in them as martyrs and victims . . . I have seen twelve-year-old boys working in chains on the public streets of Atlanta, directly in front of the schools, in company with old and hardened criminals; and this indiscriminate mingling of men and women and children makes the chain-gangs perfect schools of crime and debauchery (Du Bois, Souls of Black Folk p. 108).

Prisons and detention facilities in the U.S. are often not places for reform and transformation. In most cases, they are places where new tricks are learned, and criminal behaviors reinforced through the mingling of hardened and young criminals.

The Church of Christ is not bounded by standards of race, class, or occupation. It is not a building or an institution. It is not determined by bishops, priests, or ministers as these terms are used in their contemporary sense. Rather, the Church is God's suffering people. It is that grouping of men [women] who take seriously the words of Jesus.
(James Cone- *Black Theology and Black Power).*

The American Church:

- Provided the religious justification for slavery.[78]
- Provided the argument that the souls of Africans were inferior to Whites. Thus Black people could be easily enslaved and commercialized.
- Provided religious legitimization for the criminalization and materialization of the souls of Black people, which in turn served to legitimize the slave trade and slavery.
- Provided the religious legitimization for racism, segregation, and discrimination in the USA.
- Provided the religious claims for legalized class and racial stratification.
- The racialization of Christianity in America provided religious sanctions for the lynching of Blacks and the emergence of Jim Crow laws; precursors to mass Black incarceration.

---

[78] Joshua R. Balme, *American States, Churches and Slavery* (New York: Negro Universities Press, 1969), John Patrick Daly, *When Slavery Was Called Freedom; Evangelicalism, Proslavery and the Causes of the Civil War* (Lexington: University Press of Kentucky, 2002), Donald G. Mathews, *Slavery and Methodism: A Chapter in American Morality* 1780-1845 (Princeton, N. J.: Princeton University Press, 1965), Stephanie E. Smallwood, *Saltwater Slavery: A Middle Passage from Africa to American Diaspora* (Harvard University Press, 2008).

)

Racism and the American Criminal Justice System

Once and for all I will state this principle: A given society is
racist or it is not. Until all the evidence is available, a great
number of problems will have to be put aside.
(Frantz Fanon-*Black Skin, White Masks*).

The Bureau of Justice 2011 report states that racial discrimination in the criminal justice system has adversely influenced the sentencing process. Statistics showing people in State and Federal prisons identified by race and ethnicity reveal that Whites constituted 516, 200 (33.60%), Hispanics 349, 900 (22.80%), and Blacks 581, 300 (37.80%)[79] of the total population. Blacks are only 13% of the United States' general population. The Sentencing Project in its July 2007 analysis of racial disparity in its prison sentencing report revealed:

> Wide variation in incarceration by state, with states Northeast and Midwest exhibiting the greatest Black-to-White disparity in incarceration. In five States-Iowa, Vermont, New Jersey, Connecticut, and Wisconsin-black men are incarcerated at (a rate) more than ten times than whites.[80]

The study predicts if there is no change in this trend we should expect "one in three black males and one in six Hispanic males" going to prison, confirming the predictions of the Pew Charitable Trust quoted earlier.[81] In their article: *Criminal Justice: Race and Criminal Justice,* Ashley Nellis and her colleagues bemoan the dire effects of race in the sentencing process and the social consequences. They argue that:

---

[79] Carson, EA. Sabol, WJ, (2012) *Prisoners in 2011 Washington, D. C. Bureau of Justice Statistics.*
[80] http://www.sentencingproject.org/NewsDetails.aspx?NewsID=454
[81] Ibid.,

> Over 30 years of 'get tough,' solutions to crime in the United States have produced the world's largest prison population and incarceration rate, over 60% of whom are people of color. A large proportion of today's prisoners are victims of the failed 'War on Drugs,' which pulled in thousands of people convicted of low-level offenses for long, mandatory sentences."[82]

The War on Drugs:

"Do not accuse a man for no reason when he has done you no harm."
(Proverbs 3:30).

The American penal system disproportionally incarcerates Blacks and Hispanics for offenses associated with drug possession under the war on drugs.[83] This war employs racially based measures to prosecute Blacks and Hispanics. Drug possession and use in the Black and Hispanic communities are considered criminal offenses.[84] On the other hand, Whites caught with drugs are not often considered criminals; their drug possession and use are often considered a health problem. A particular example is a laxity with which Methamphetamine (Meth) users receive lesser sentences because a lot of Meth users are White. On the other hand, crack

---

[82] Criminal Justice: *Race and Criminal in Compact for Racial Justice: An Agenda for Fairness and United* (A proactive plan for fairness and unity in our communities, politics, the economy and the law, Applied Research Center) rd_compact_final.pdf, 17 (Accessed: 01/31/09).

[83] http://www.sentencingproject.org/NewsDetails.aspx?NewsID=4549: rd_crisisoftheyoung[1].pdf "While the numbers of inmates in the federal prison system are smaller overall, the scale of the increase has been similar. The 4,900 federal drug offenders in 1980 represented 25% of the inmate population. This grew to 51,700, or 60%, by 1995. Looking at prisons and jails combined, there are now an estimated 400, 000 inmates either awaiting trial or serving time for a drug offense, out of a total inmate population of 1.7million. As these policies are implemented, they have increasingly affected African American and Hispanic communities. The African American proportion of drug arrests has risen from 25% in 1980 to 37% in 1995. Hispanic and African American inmates are more likely than non-Hispanic whites to be incarcerated for a drug offense. As of 1991, 33% of Hispanic state prison inmates had been convicted of a drug offense, 25% of blacks, 12% of non-Hispanic whites."

[84] Data Show Racial Disparity in Crack Sentencing

cocaine, supposedly used by Blacks only is highly criminalized with tough sentences while powder cocaine, supposedly used by Whites carries a lesser sentence. Meth and powder cocaine used predominantly by Whites receive lesser sentences or rehabilitation while crack cocaine, used by Blacks is highly criminalized with Black users receiving higher three-strikes sentences of longer prison time. The White person is most often referred to a rehabilitation program, while Blacks and Hispanics are criminalized, given maximum sentences, and incarcerated. According to the Drug Policy Alliance 2016 report, *The Drug War, Mass Incarceration, and Race,* Blacks and Hispanics experience "discrimination at every stage of the judicial system are more likely to be stopped, searched, arrested, convicted, harshly sentenced and saddled with a lifelong criminal record." [85]   Drug sentences show the extent of racial disparity in the US penal system. It reports that Blacks "comprise 31 percent of those arrested for drug law violations and nearly 40 percent of those incarcerated in state or federal prison for drug law violations."[86] The disparities in the use of various kinds of illegal drugs by Blacks, Whites, and Hispanics particularly have become quite evident. According to Saki Knafo, White Americans use more illegal drugs like cocaine, LSD, and marijuana than Blacks but Blacks face longer prison sentences than Whites. He writes:

> Nearly 20 percent of whites have used cocaine, compared with 10 percent of blacks and Latinos, according to a 2011 survey from the Substance Abuse and Mental Health Services Administration. Higher percentages of whites have also tried hallucinogens, marijuana, pain relievers like OxyContin, and stimulants like methamphetamine. Still, blacks are arrested for drug possession more than three times as often as whites...Of the 225,242 people who were serving time in state prisons for drug offenses, in

---

[85] Drug Policy Alliance, *The Drug War, Mass Incarceration and Race,* p. 1.
[86] Drug Policy Alliance, *The Drug War, Mass Incarceration and Race,* p. 1.

2011, blacks made up 45 percent and whites comprised just 30 percent.[87]

Disparity associated with drug sentencing is especially obvious when looking at the rates of arrest and incarceration of those associated with marijuana cases. A 2013 report by the ACLU argues that the over 40 years of US domestic war on drugs has been a failure with collateral consequences for the lives of its victims and communities. With over 40 million arrests and over billions of dollars used to incarcerate Americans with Blacks and their communities particularly affected. It contends that the war on drugs has been a "war on people of color" in the United States. Not only is the war target oriented, but it is also selectively enforced against Blacks and their communities.

> In 2010, the Black arrest rate for marijuana possession was 716 per 100,000, while the white arrest rate was 192 per 100,000. Stated another way, a Black person was 3.73 times more likely to be arrested for marijuana possession than a white person — a disparity that increased 32.7% between 2001 and 2010. It is not surprising that the War on Marijuana, waged with far less fanfare than the earlier phases of the drug war, has gone largely, if not entirely, unnoticed by middle- and upper-class white communities.[88]

The ACLU report further contends that the selective nature of the war on drugs is particularly high in states and counties where the Black population is less than other racial groups. Blacks, nonetheless, experience higher rates of arrest and incarceration for marijuana possession. It contends that Law enforcement authorities including the police have for over four decades targeted minority

---

[87] Saki Knafo, *When it Comes to Illegal Drug Use, White America Does the Crime, Black America Gets the Time*, (The Huffington Post, http://www.huffingtonpost.com/2013/09/17/racial-disparity-drug-use_n_3941346.html)
[88] American Civil Liberties Union, *The War on Marijuana In Black and White*, p. 9.

communities thus resulting in the unusual rates of Black incarceration in the United States.

> In the states with the worst disparities, Blacks were on average over six times more likely to be arrested for marijuana possession than whites. In the worst offending counties across the country, Blacks were over 10, 15, even 30 times more likely to be arrested than white residents in the same county. These glaring racial disparities in marijuana arrests are not a northern or southern phenomenon, nor a rural or urban phenomenon, but rather a national one.[89]

The Sentencing Project confirms the ACLU's conclusion that the American war on drugs is racially selective and enforced against Blacks. It contends that Blacks face enormous obstacles in the American penal system when facing a judge or prosecutor regarding the possession of any illegal drug in contrast to White possessors and users. According to the Sentencing Project,

> The prosecution of the drug war has disproportionately affected communities of color. Surveys conducted by the Department of Health and Human Services estimate that blacks constitute 13.3% of monthly drug users, yet blacks represent 32.5% of persons arrested for drug offenses. Of all persons imprisoned for drug offenses, three-fourths are blacks or Latino. These disparities result in large part through a two-tiered application of the drug war. In communities with substantial resources, drug abuse is primarily addressed as a public health problem utilizing prevention and treatment approaches. In low-income communities, those resources are in short supply and drug

---

[89] American Civil Liberties Union, *The War on Marijuana In Black and White*, p. 9

problems are more likely to be addressed through the criminal justice system.[90]

In 2001, a reported indicated that only 13% of Blacks were known to have used drugs, but were disproportionately incarcerated for drug offenses more than any other minority group.[91] Most crack cocaine users are White, but Blacks face harsh sentences than Whites for drug offenses.[92]

According to Marc Mauer, director of the Sentencing Project, between the 1970s and 2007, the incarceration rate increased to 500% with approximately 2.2 million individuals imprisoned across the country.[93] Blacks make up more than one million of this amount.[94] For Mauer, the national picture on "substantial racial disparity" reflects a deep racial consciousness evident in the American prison system.

> The American prison and jail system is defined by an entrenched racial disparity in the population of incarcerated people. The national incarceration rate for whites is 412 per 100,000 residents, compared to 2, 290 for African Americans

---

[90] www.Sentencingproject.org/rd_brownvboard[1].pdf (Substances Abuse and Mental Health Service Administration, Office of Applied Studies, National Survey on Drug Use and Health, 2002. Table 1. 26A) 3. (Accessed 2/04/2008)

[91] Ibid. "In the first five years after the passage of the Omnibus Anti-Drug Act of 1986, African Americans accounted for more than 80 percent of the increase in incarcerated drug offenders. In state facilities during that period, the rate of black citizens incarcerated increased by 465. 5 percent, compared to a 110.6 percent increase for whites. One may guess that this disparity is due to extremely high drug use by blacks, but according to the US Sentencing Commission, only 13 percent of all drug users are blacks which match their percent in the population."

[92] www.sentencingproject.org/women_cjs_overview (1). "A 1992 study showed that no white defendants had been prosecuted federally on crack charges in 17 states and many cities. Only one white person had been convicted in federal courts in California, two in Texas, three in New York and two in Pennsylvania. This is in spite of the fact that many people believe that most crack cocaine users are black but according to federal surveys, most crack cocaine users are white (a 1995 report put the figure at 52 percent)." (Accessed 2/08/2008)

[93] The Sentencing Project: *"Uneven Justice: State Rates of Incarceration by Race and Ethnicity,"* Marc Mauer and Ryan S. King, July 2007 (rd_stateratesofincbyraceandethnicity[1].pdf.

[94] Ibid 5(rd_stateratesofincbyraceandethnicity[1].pdf.

and 742 for Hispanics. These figures mean that 2.3% of all
African Americans are incarcerated, compared to 0.4% of
whites and 0.7% of Hispanics."

Furthermore, "while these overall rates of incarceration are
all at record highs, they fail to reflect the concentrated impact
of incarceration among young African American males in
particular, many of whom reside in disadvantaged
neighborhoods. One in nine (11.7%) African-American
males between the ages of 25 and 29 are currently
incarcerated in a prison or jail.[95]

Furthermore, Blacks and Hispanics charged with drug possession
are penalized with harsher three-strike sentences. Three-strikes
sentences carry longer prison time.[96]

Pat Nolan reflects on the toil of a longer sentence. Nolan was
a Republican legislator with a long political career and well
connected. His résumé shows he went to law school at USC Law
School. But in the 1990s, Nolan was convicted and imprisoned.
Before his imprisonment, Nolan was an avid advocate for harsher
prison time. Unfortunately, he was caught receiving checks from an
undercover agent of the FBI and sentenced to twenty-six months.
While in prison, he got converted, and upon his release, he became
a champion of reformed and better treatment for prisoners in the
criminal justice system. Nolan experienced a reality check together
with his conversion experience; it was the sober reality of
depersonalization and hopelessness. He describes his experience as
follows:

You're an amputee, cut off from family, community, job,
church, and, with your stump still bleeding, you're tossed into
this boiling cauldron of anger, hatred, bitterness, sexual
repression, and you're totally disrespected—screamed at—by

---

[95] Ibid 4 (rd_stateratesofincbyraceandethnicity[1].pdf
[96] James Austin, John Clark, Particia Hardyman and Alan Henry, *Three Strikes and You're Out:
The Implementation and Impart of Strike Laws,*
(https://www.ncjrs.gov/pdffiles1/nij/grants/181297.pdf) p. 2.

officers all the time . . .You are sneered at with venom and told repeatedly, "You ain't got anything coming."

The implication is that you are nothing, you've come from nothing and you will be nothing. You are worthless. You have no future. None . . . As a legislator, I had assumed that our prisons were not only preparing people for success upon release, but also helping these damaged men develop a moral compass, and ensuring that they analyzed the bad decisions that got them in trouble, I was wrong.[97]

Since his release, Nolan has committed his life to prison reform.[98] Nolan articulates an existential experience associated with imprisonment that has now become the norm for Black men, youths and women, and their communities. With the latest report, Blacks are 13% of the general population of the United States but account for 51% of the prison population.

The notion that Blacks are more violent contributing in several ways to the high rate of detention and incarceration.[99] This assumption, per most legal analysts, is a misnomer. Police bias and prejudice have contributed to the disproportion in the incarceration

---

[97] http://www.latimes.com/news/local/la-me-nolan5ju105,1, 2867656,f

[98] http://www.hrw.org/reports/2000/usa/Rcedrg00-01.htm sees this document for detail: "The disproportionate representation of Black Americans in the U.S. criminal justice system is well documented. Blacks comprise 13 percent of the national population, but 30 percent of people arrested, 41 percent of people in jail, and 49 percent of those in prison. Nine percent of all black adults are under some form of correctional supervision (in jail or prison, on probation or parole), compared to two percent of white adults. One in three black men between the ages of 20 and 29 was either in jail or prison, or on parole or probation in 1995. One in ten black men in their twenties and early thirties is in prison or jail. Thirteen percent of the black adult male population has lost the right to vote because of felony disenfranchisement laws."

[99] p. 37; Parenti, p. 11 www. sentencingproject.org/women_cjs_ overview(1)[1].pdf

rates of Blacks.[100] Black youths are treated differently than White youths with similar offense records in the juvenile justice system.[101]

Structural Causes of Mass Incarceration:

The quest for the Negro male for employment was always frustrating. If he lacked skill, he was only occasionally wanted because such employment as he could find had little regularity and even less remuneration. If he had a skill, he also had his black skin, and discrimination locked doors against him. In the competition for scarce job he was a loser because he was born that way.
(Martin Luther King, Jr. *Where Do We Go from Here: Chaos or Community?* p. 106).

Mass incarceration systematically creates and perpetuates conditions of poverty, the breakdown of family structures, community insecurity and undermines public safety. The

---

[100] www.sentencingproject.org/women_cjs_overview(1)[1].pdf "Hindelang (1978) attempted to assess the extent to which black overrepresentation in arrest statistics reflects differential involvement by blacks in crime or differential selection of blacks for arrest by the police. He compared FBI arrest statistics for common-law, personal crimes with the racial identification of offenders made by victims of the National Victimization Panel. While finding some evidence of police bias, he concluded that the data for rape, robbery and assault are generally consistent with official data on arrests and support the differential involvement hypothesis. As further evidence in support of the differential involvement hypothesis for black overrepresentation in arrest statistics, Silverman (1978) reported that Puerto Rican New Yorkers, who are, as a group, poorer and less educated than black New Yorkers, have only one-third the arrest rate of blacks for violent crimes. Mexican Americans in south Texas have one-eighth the conviction rate of black Texans for robbery."

[101] Ibid., "According to the Justice Department's study, among white youth offenders, 66% are referred to juvenile courts, while only 31% of the African American youth are taken there. Blacks comprise 44% of those detained in juvenile jail, 46% of all those tried in adult criminal courts, as well as 58% of all juveniles who are warehoused in adult prison. This means that for young African Americans who are arrested and charged with a crime, they are six times more likely to be assigned to prisons than white youth offenders."

Sentencing Project argues that the following conditions are inherent to the growth of mass incarceration.

Education:

- Poor quality education and illiteracy.
- Black youths make up the highest number of those placed in Special Education Programs.
- Lack of access to quality education.
- The high rates of high school dropout.

Family:

- Dysfunctional family structures.
- Lack of access to transition to "adult roles."
- Incarceration as a normative experience for most Black men and the Black community.[102]

Crime and punishment:

- The high number of Black juveniles in the Department of Youth Services or DYS.
- Extreme emphasis on punitive measures rather than rehabilitation.[103]

---

[102] *American Sociological Review*, 2004, Vol. 69 (April: 151-169), Mass_ Imprisonment_and_the_life_Race_and_Class_Ineq[1].pdf p 151 "High incarceration rates led researchers to claim that prison time had become a normal part of the early adulthood for black men in poor urban neighborhoods."

[103] www.Sentencingproject.org/rd_brownvboard[1].pdf, p. 2 "Crime Rate: Higher rates of involvement in some crimes explain part of the high rate of black imprisonment. For property offenses, blacks constituted 29% of arrests in 2002 and for violent offenses, 38%; these compared to the 12.3 % black proportion of the total population. (Note that an arrest may not always be an accurate indicator of involvement in crime, but it often remains the best means of approximating this measure). However, criminologist Alfred Blumstein, in a study on race and imprisonment, noted that higher arrest rates for drugs crimes in particular were not correlated with higher rates of use in the general population. In short, drug arrest

- Allegedly, higher crime rates in the Black community.
- States with large White population and small Black population tend to have the highest rates of Black incarceration and detention.[104]

Indications of "Concentrated" poverty

- Low-income, lack of career skills and unemployment.[105]
- Systemic "socio-economic disadvantages."[106]
- The degree of poverty characterized by dilapidated city environment and, homelessness.
- High infant mortality rates.
- Poor housing environment.
- The number of Blacks living in ghetto areas increased to 38 percent.[107]
- Unemployment before an arrest is also a large factor.

As previously indicated, the criminalization of Black men in America continues to be a major organizing factor. Criminalization engenders arbitrary arrests and harsher punitive measures. Criminalization as an impetus maintains the crime statistics because

---

patterns were not a reliable indicator of drug offending, because African-Americans are arrested more frequently than their rate of drug use would suggest" (Blumstein, Alfred. (1993). "Racial Disproportionality of U.S. Prison Population Revisited," *University of Colorado Law Review*, Vol. 64, 743-760).

[104] American Sociological Review, 2004, Vol. 69 (April: 151-169), 153 "Strongest evidence for racially differential treatment is found for some offenses and in some jurisdictions rather than a t the aggregate level. African Americans are at especially high risk of incarceration, given their arrest rates, for drugs crimes and burglary. States with large white populations also tend to incarcerate blacks at a high rate, controlling for race-specific arrest rates and demographic variables. A large residual racial disparity in imprisonment thus appears due to the differential treatment of African Americans by police and the courts."

[105] Ibid., 3.
[106] Ibid., 3.
[107] Ibid., 3-5.

it presents Black men as perpetual criminals. In maintaining the statistics by whatever means possible, the Black person's sense of personhood is disregarded and distorted in the eyes of every citizen and visitor who comes to the United States. In perpetuating the stereotype that Black men are criminals and, therefore, must be detained and incarcerated, a notion that the Black man as inherently suspicious thus subjecting him to arbitrary arrest. The criminalization of Black men makes it difficult for most Black men to experience economic mobility without their subjection to racial scrutiny. The situation is worse for those with a criminal record. The disempowerment of the Black man in America is often due to his criminalization, his profiling and arbitrary arrest, his sentencing, detention, incarceration and the racialization of his crime rather than dealing with the crime itself.[108]

Main Points:

- The war on drugs is a racial war.
- The war on drug targets minority men, women, and youths.
- Whites use more illegal drugs than Blacks, but Blacks get more jail and prison time.
- Blacks and Hispanics in possession and use of illegal drugs are criminalized.
- Whites in possession and use of illegal drugs receive lesser prison time and higher access to rehabilitation programs.

---

[108] Jennifer C. Karberg, and Beck, Allen J. *"Trends in U.S. Correctional Populations: Findings from the Bureau of Justice Statistics."* Presented at the National Committee on Community Corrections Meeting, Washington, DC, and April 16, 2004.

Social Consequences
Breakdown of the Black Family Structure

The underprivileged everywhere have long since abandoned any hope that this type of salvation deals with the crucial issues by which their days are turned into despair without consolation.
(Howard Thurman, *Jesus and the Disinherited*, Pg. 29-30).

The large-scale imprisonment of Black men also has its social consequences. For the Black man, it reflects his disempowerment. One of the consequences of mass incarceration is the grave experience of economic dependency and marginalization for adult Black males and women with felony records. It is a kind of dependency that leads to intergenerational impoverishment. Economic dependency leads to economic marginalization often reflected in the lives of the children of the prisoner or former prisoner. The lack of income leads to deep frustration and anxiety. In many cases, Black men take their own lives or do something to return to prison which also accounts for the high rate of recidivism among minority men and women.

This cycle of confinement reflects the dilemma of the Black man. Imprisoned in his teens, he must stay in jail, imprisonment, or detention until he is an adult. Unfortunately, if he did not complete high school before his arrest, he is at a great disadvantage upon his release. He lacks the social and employment skills necessary to support himself in the society. Furthermore, society expects him to be a good citizen, but according to Hegel's view of crime and punishment, he is right-less. If we examine Hegel's assertion, we realize that in its literal interpretation, the Black man with a criminal record will always be considered a criminal in America. Because of his crime, he can no longer be a viable participant in and contributor to the society. His crime nullifies both his inherent right and his concrete right as a citizen since the crime committed is an "infinite injury." But as a Black man, he was a suspect even before his crime.

According to Hegel, when one commits a crime, he must pay the due penalty for his crime, but after paying the due penalty for his crime, he remains a criminal for life even if his punishment was pardoned. The fact that he must remain a criminal after serving his time, and denied housing, voting rights, etc. is very disturbing and unjust.[109] For the Black man, his criminalization precedes him. He is criminalized before committing a crime, and when he commits a crime, his crime induces harsher punishment because his crime is associated with his racial identity. Like himself, his crime is racialized. He cannot easily get a job even if he is employable; he cannot easily buy a home. It is almost impossible to receive federal aid if he wants to go to school, he cannot work for the government, and he cannot participate in the political process of his country because of his felony record, not his punishment, disqualifies him from voting.[110] He has already served his time, but he is still a criminal. In 2001, 13% of all Black men could not vote because of their records. That number is approximately 1.4 million.

He has served his time in prison but remains a criminal and a criminal for life: A Black criminal, not just a criminal. The existential experience of the formerly incarcerated in the U.S, especially if he or she is Black, is a classic case of marginalization and intergenerational impoverishment. The Black man's crime is associated with his racial identity. There are many in this situation, and most of them are Black men and women.

The social consequences are felt on different levels.[111] The impact of over a million Black men and youths in prisons and jails across the U.S. leads to dysfunctional family structures, fatherlessness, and Black boys growing up without role models in many Black homes.[112] According to Mauer the "ripple effect" of the increase in the

---

[109] Hegel, PR. 282.

[110] http://www.sentencingproject.org/issueAreaHome.aspx?IssueID=4.

[111] www.Sentencingproject.org/rd_brownvboard[1].pdf. 5

[112] Ibid., 5 "One of every 14 black children has a parent in prison on any given day; over the course of childhood, the figures would be much higher. Family formation, particularly in urban areas heavily affected by incarceration, is also affected by these trends. In the highest incarceration neighborhoods of Washington, D.C., the absence of black men has created a gender ratio of only 62 men for every 100 women."

incarceration of Black men has systematically affected the Black family structure. He writes:

> The rate of incarceration for African Americans in the United States is now at a level that is seriously affecting life prospect for the generation of black children growing up today. In addition, the ripple effects of current policy now extend the impact of incarceration beyond just the individual in prison, but to families and communities as well.[113]

It provides a perfect opportunity that gangs have capitalized upon by providing "protection," "financial security," a "sense of belonging," and "self-confidence."[114]

BLACK WOMEN BEHIND BARS

Prison is not an effective remedy for the drug addiction and economic distress that contribute to the crimes women commit. It makes much more sense to address the root issues by providing community-based drug treatment and investing in alternatives to incarceration.
(Women's Prison Association, 2007).

---

[113] Marc Mauer, rd_racialimpactstatements.pdf, 46, (Accessed 01/31/09)

[114] Ibid., 12, 1999. rd_crisisoftheyoung [1].pdf "It is likely that the prison population overall will continue to grow in coming years. A survey of state correction agencies found that state officials projected that the 1994 prison population would rise by 51% by the year 2000. Despite falling crime rates, a variety of sentencing policies adopted in the past Fifteen years are contributing to the burgeoning of the prison population. These include the mandatory sentencing laws now in effect in all fifty states and the federal system, the 'three-strikes-and-you're-out' law in nearly half the states, and newly-adopted 'truth sentencing' policies that will increase the time served in prison for many offenders by requiring that they serve 85% of their sentence. Preliminary indications of this trend are already evident in research by the Bureau of Justice Statistics, which show that the percentage served prior to release increased from 38% in 1990 to 44% in 1996."

45

According to the Sentencing Project,

> Over the past quarter century, there has been a profound change in the involvement of women within the criminal justice system. This is the result of more expansive law enforcement efforts, stiffer drug sentencing laws, and post-conviction barriers to reentry that uniquely affect women. Women now comprise a larger proportion of the prison population than ever before; the female prison population stands nearly eight times higher than its population count in 1980. More than 60% of women in state prisons have a child under the age of 18...Between 1980 and 2014, the number of incarcerated women increased by more than 700%, rising from a total of 26,378 in 1980 to 215,332 in 2014.[115]

Blacks are 13% of the general population of the United States. It is important that this general percentage be taken into consideration if interpreting the disproportionality associated with race and incarceration in the United States. According to the Sentencing Project:

Race and Ethnicity statistics on female incarceration rates:

- In 2014, the imprisonment rate for African American women (109 per 100,000) was more than twice the rate of imprisonment for white women (53 per 100,000).
- Hispanic women were incarcerated at 1.2 times the rate of white women (64 vs. 53 per 100,000).
- The rate of imprisonment for African American women has been declining since 2000, while the rate of imprisonment for white women continues to rise.
- Between 2000 and 2014, the rate of imprisonment in state and federal prisons declined by 47% for black

---

[115] The Sentencing Project: Incarcerated Women and Girls:
http://www.sentencingproject.org/publications/incarcerated-women-and-girls/

women, while the rate of imprisonment for white women rose by 56%.[116]

Black men (over 43%) and Black women consist of the highest number of those incarcerated in the United States prison system. The Sentencing Project fact sheet on *Incarcerated Women* states that:

> The number of women in prison increased by 646% between 1980 and 2010, rising from 15,118 to 112,797, including women in local jails; more than 205,000 women are now incarcerated.
> The number of women in prison increased at nearly 1.5 times the rate of men (646% versus 419%).
> As of 2010, more than 1 million women were under the supervision of the criminal justice system.

- **Prison 112,7973**
- **Jail 93,3004**
- **Probation 712,0845**
- **Parole 103,3746**
- **The configuration of the above numbers is puzzling.**

The lifetime likelihood of imprisonment for women is 1 in 56; however, the chance of a woman imprisoned varies by race. As of 2001, the lifetime likelihood of female imprisonment was the following:

- **1 in 19 for Black women**
- **1 in 45 for Hispanic women**
- **1 in 118 for White women**

In 2010, Black women were incarcerated at nearly three times the rate of white women (133 versus 47 per 100,000).

---

[116] The Sentencing Project: Incarcerated Women and Girls:
http://www.sentencingproject.org/publications/incarcerated-women-and-girls/

Hispanic women were incarcerated at 1.6 times the rate of white women (77 versus 47 per 100,000).[117]

The mass incarceration of Black fathers and Black mothers, and in several cases, children, in the U.S. prison system, has fundamentally led to the development of dysfunctional family structures and the breakdown of families. It is also possible to argue that mass incarceration is an immediate source of Black-on-Black crime and Black homicide. The moral and ethical debilitations associated with this rate of incarceration and condoned in the United States' criminal justice system is unprecedented in any country in the world. In the United States' criminal justice system, Black men and Black women receive the longest, most punitive, and the most maximum sentences for both violent and non-violent crimes than their White and Hispanic counterparts. Mass Black incarceration in the United States is an existential dilemma for the Black community. That the American criminal justice system has considered normative, this rate of incarcerating human beings is disturbing. According to the Sentencing Project:

> The likelihood that children will have parents who are incarcerated is disproportionately linked to race. In 1990, one of every 14 black children had a parent in prison, compared with one in every 125 white children. Black children are almost (more) likely than white children to have a parent in prison and Hispanic children are 3 times more likely.[118]

Concerning mothers behind bars in the United States' prison system, the Sentencing Project fact sheet on *Incarcerated Women* concludes from its research that:

> Women in state prisons are more likely to have minor children than are men (62% versus 51%).

---

[117] The Sentencing Project: *Incarcerated Women.*
http://www.sentencingproject.org/doc/publications/cc_Incarcerated_Women_Factsheet_Sep24sp.pdf
[118] www.sentencingproject.org/women_cjs_overview(1) [1].pdf.

> 64% of mothers in state prisons lived with their children before they were sent to prison compared to 47% of fathers.
>
> Mothers in prison are more likely than fathers to have children living with grandparents (45% versus 13%), other relatives (23% versus 5%), or in foster care (11% versus 2%).
>
> 1 in 25 women in state prisons and 1 in 33 in federal prisons are pregnant when admitted to prison.
>
> Women can be shackled during labor and delivery in all but 13 states.
>
> Most children born to incarcerated mothers are immediately separated from their mothers.[119]

Thus, we are beginning to witness the systemic disintegration of the Black family structure in the 21st century in the United States as a result of the mass incarceration of Black men, Black women, and Black juveniles.

According to Pope John Paul II, the family is a very important institution in the society. It is the child's first introduction to life and love as "stabilizing influences" for society and the Church. He writes,

> It is the first and irreplaceable school of life, an example and stimulus for the broader community relationships marked by respect, justice dialogue, and love . . . The family is thus . . . the place of origin and the most effective means for humanizing and personalizing society: it makes an original contribution in depth to building up the world, by making possible a life that is possibly speaking human, in particular by guarding and transmitting virtues and "values."[120]

---

[119] The Sentencing Project: *Incarcerated Women*:
http://www.sentencingproject.org/doc/publications/cc_Incarcerated_Women_Factsheet_S ep24sp.pdf
[120] Familiaris Consortio, 43.

The breakdown of the Black family structure due to disproportionate rates of incarceration is not a recent development. King argues that the Black family has been historically "scarred" and "disorganized" in the United States. The process of disorganization he further argues goes back to slavery. The basic difference between immigrants' and the historic American Black family is that Blacks were brought in "chains when they arrived on these shores."[121] The elements of choice, free will and volition were not entertained. He writes: "Above all, no other ethnic group has been a slave on American soil, and no other group has had its family structure deliberately torn apart. This is the rub."[122] King explains that Black families were sold on auction blocks as their initial experience on the shores of America. Marriages were considered illegal for slaves, though the slave master "might direct mating" with the existence of "fragile monogamous relationships." What was most disturbing, he writes was:

> Repetitive tearing apart of families as children, husbands or wives were sold to other plantations. But these cruel conditions were not yet the whole story. Masters and their sons used Negro women to satisfy their spontaneous lust or, when more humane attitudes prevailed, as concubines. The depth were reached in Virginia... There slaves were bred for sales, not casually or incidentally, but in a vast deliberate program which produced enormous wealth for slaveowners. This breeding program was one answer to the legal halting of the slave traffic early in the nineteenth century. [123]

King intimates that despite these treatments of family horror, the Black family has managed to survive. These historical antipathies towards Black identity and family relationship have left the Black family "fragile, deprived and often psychopathic" with the absence of long-

---

[121] King, 1968, p. 103.
[122] King, 1968, p. 103.
[123] King, 1968, p. 104.

term security, safety net, and community. Thus leaving the "future bleak, if not hopeless." [124] The disproportionate rate of Black incarceration and its impact on the Black family structure thus reflect a continuity from the fragility of the Black family structure from slavery to the present.

In the case of Blacks considered illegal and deported, family responsibilities often fall on the wife. Take for instance the case of Georgina and Howard Facey.

Georgina, an African American, and Howard, a Jamaican, got married in 1997 and gave birth to four children who are American citizens. Georgina filed immigration papers for her husband immediately. Unfortunately, it took six years before they heard anything about the case. At the advice of a lawyer, Howard went to the immigration office at Federal Plaza in New York to inquire about his papers but in the process was arrested upon his inquiry. He was detained and processed for deportation to Jamaica. They did not give him the opportunity to see a judge. According to Georgina,

> Howard called home from JFK airport at 6:00 a.m. to say that he was being deported. My heart sank, but I did not have the time to break down. I had to get our three kids ready for school and rush to work at a local drugstore. Letisha, Kristina, and Christopher ask for their dad every day. Their grades are dropping, and the school counselor says they are depressed. Childcare is really hard. When a family friend who was supposed to get Christopher from school was late a few times, the principal threatened to call Children's Services. With all this pressure, I don't have the time to properly treat my heart condition . . . Back . . . in the Caribbean, no one will hire a U.S. deportee.[125]

In a statement, Howard narrates his ordeal:

> I went to Federal Plaza to pick up my work forms. When I went before "a few months ago," they told me to just come back and

---

[124] King, 1968, p. 107.
[125] www.familiesoffreedom.org April 2, 2008 at 8:00 p.m.

things would be ready. The forms were ready, but the officers would not give them to me. They told me I had some errors years ago. I did not really know what they were talking about. But they shackled my hands and feet and put a chain around my waist. Then they sent me over to a jail for a few days, and then to the airport. I felt so awful. I couldn't believe it . . . I long to be with my girls.[126]

During the ordeal, Georgina did not give up. She writes, "On Wednesday we are going to our Congressman Ed Towns to ask for help. We are also going to our Senators. We vote them into office to protect our families. Hopefully, our Congressman and Senators can help reunite my family soon."[127] The year was 2004. Hopefully, Howard may have joined his family back in the United States. I accessed this story from the Families of Freedom Web site.

Imprisonment Is Not a Rite of Passage

Instead of building schools and housing and workplaces for the poor, we build them jails-at far greater cost. Instead of intervening early to help children born with two strikes against them, we ignore them until we can say with perverted glee, 'Strike three! You're out![128]
(James Carroll in his 1994 commentary).

A culture of arrest and mass incarceration for any group of people eventually transforms itself into their worldview. The experience becomes a shared experience in the community. In this context, instead of the Black child experiencing a normal and steady introduction to society and societal values, raised with the consciousness of participating in society, he is raised by the

---

[126] Ibid.,

[127] Ibid.,

[128] Carroll, James "*Is It Time to Dismantle the Revenge Machine?*" Boston Globe 3 (February 8 1994) p. 19 (03/14/2009).

experience and consciousness of a subculture that makes little allowance for a proper social development. The consequences are profound. He might think incarceration connotes manliness and dominance. Thus, his paradigm for life and success is skewed, and his sense of progress distorted. His ability to properly behave in society and by societal norms is impaired. His life is transformed by the shared experience of mass incarceration. The Black child that grows up in this environment perceives incarceration as a badge of honor especially when his father and brothers have shared incarceration experience. The assumption is that one has done something to deserve recognition. He has "graduated" into "manhood." For many Black youths, imprisonment has become a part of their maturing process.

> The approaches taken (imprisonment and racially formulated forms of policy implementation) to address this problem over the past several decades have created a situation whereby imprisonment has come to be seen as an almost inevitable aspect of the maturing process for black men, and increasingly for black women.[129]

While individual and family responsibilities largely ought to minimize the negative perception of the society on the growth of the child, we see the same family structure is influenced by the social consciousness of negativity in most Black neighborhoods. Per available data, "A black male born in 1991 has a 29% chance of spending time in prison at some point in his life. The figure for white males is 4% and for Hispanics 16%."[130]

Blacks easily acquire criminal records because they are Black; the socio-historical consciousness of the society informs and enforces the consciousness that Black men are criminals. Mark

---

[129] www.Sentencingproject.org/rd_brownvboard[1].pdf5.

[130] Maier, Marc, *The Crisis of the Young African American Male and the Criminal Justice System*, (D.C, prepared for the U.S. Commission on Civil Rights, April 15-16, 1999), rd_crisisoftheyoung[1].pdf p. 3

Mauer of the Sentencing Project notes, "Offenses by blacks are more likely to lead to arrest than those of whites. While the self-reported involvement of adolescent males represents a 3:2 Black/White deferential, the arrest ratio is 4:1."[131]

Why should incarceration be viewed as a rite of passage? It is because the Black youth is stereotyped before he can define his reality. He is conscious of the feeling of being an outsider because of his race and skin color, even though an "insider." Without the opportunity for normal social development into adulthood, the slightest misbehavior is considered deviant and intellectually inferior. He is sent to DYS or placed in a special education category, and there he finds it difficult to progress on to college. But this is the beginning of his demise and the shattering of his evolving world. As a Black youth, a judge may not look kindly on him to understand his background, but may quickly sentence him to an adult prison where an even more distorted process of mental and psychological development takes place among hardened criminals. His life is on the verge of destruction and his potential and zest for life twisted as he leaves the prison walls with a distorted self-image and worldview.

He confronts an economic dilemma upon his release from prison. He might not have completed high school and might not have learned any employable skill behind bars. He comes out uneducated, unskilled, and untrained and lost in the world. His only option is to depend on his natural strength, which renders him susceptible to violence, crime, abuse, and self-destruction. In the absence of supportive resources, his chances for success in life continue to narrow, and thus, imprisonment no longer becomes a choice but the only option to avoid his woes.

Not only is he confronted with an economic dilemma, but also a political dilemma. His rights as a citizen were eclipsed before he came to the consciousness of it. When he came to understand that he had rights, they were gone. His innocence and naivety were not pardoned. He must now live right-less as a citizen. He ends up becoming a liability, but he must still pay his dues to society; yet, he

---

[131] Ibid., 3.

finds it difficult to be employed, and he cannot survive independently. He is right-less and finds it difficult to be responsible for a wife, a child, and a family. It is difficult to find a job to provide for his family because he served time in jail for a crime he committed or did not commit. He served the time but must be stigmatized, especially as a Black man. The system disempowers him as a man. Now he must forever abide by the rules of other men who like him are citizens, but unlike him, have rights. This is the dilemma of the incarcerated minority man and woman.

He must tell himself like the Psalmist, "I shall not die but live," "God is my refuge and strength, an ever-present help in time of trouble." His only source of hope is the "Spark of the Divine" within us, which stubbornly pulls us toward the source of our being. There is a multitude of men and women caught in this anxiety, this anarchy, and bewilderment within. Some have nowhere to go and no one to run to; they must return to imprisonment. How painful this must be.[132]

'Dirty nigger!' Or Simply, 'Look, a Negro!' I came into the world imbued with the will to find a meaning in things, my spirit filled with the desire to attain to the source of the world, and then I found that I was an object in the midst of other objects.
(Frantz Fanon-*Black Skin, White Masks, p.109).*

A problematic assumption that also informs the sociopolitical and economic consciousness is the constant attempt to equate crime and criminality with poverty: That the poor person is a criminal and that poverty implies moral and ethical incontinence. In this case, the poor are susceptible to every form of suspicion.[133] It is the argument that

---

[132] *American Sociological Review*, 2004, Vol. 69 (April: 151-169), Mass_ Imprisonment_ and _the _life_Race_and_Class_Ineq [1].pdf. 156

[133] Arthur L. Rizer 111, *The Race Effect On Wrongful Convictions: Rizer Article formatted Current. Doc*, 7_Rizer [1].pdf, William Mitchell Law Review, Vol. 29:3 p 848. (Susan H. Bitensky, Section 1983: *Agent of Peace or Vehicle of Violence Against Children*, 54 OKLA. L. Rev. 333, 372 n.61 (2001); Constance R. LeSage, *The Death Penalty for Rape-Cruel and Unusual Punishment?* 38 LA. L. Rev. 868, 870 n.8 (1978).

the poor are poor because they are immoral and lazy. The rich are rich because they are moral and ethical. This is a fallacious assumption. I reject the argument that the rich should be catered to and protected against the poor and that the poor are criminals, threats to society, the trouble rousers, the disturbers of the peace, dependent on the government, and should, therefore, be penalized. To support such an assumption is to constantly reduce the poor to stereotypes of criminality, intellectual inferiority, and racism. The color of their skin, the shape of their eyes, and the texture of their hair, the spelling of their names, their accent, their intelligence, and their connections are thus used to judge and define them.

There are rich criminals, but the nexus between grinding poverty and crime levels is beyond dispute. The gross disproportion of ethnic minorities within the prison population reflects not simply the racial prejudice found among law officers and the judiciary but also the systemic racism that drives ethnic minorities towards the bottom of social hierarchies. So much crime among disadvantaged groups is drug-related, and that reflects both the use of drugs to cope with an inhumane existence and even more the attraction of making quick money by peddling drugs when other sources of income are not easily available. To argue that social deprivation and criminality are the only organizing causes for incarceration do not lessen the reality of racism. Social deprivation and criminality are part of the impact of racism.

No matter how simple the differences are, given our common humanity, they are elevated to define the destiny of an ethnic group. The material identity of the ethnic group becomes the immediate yardstick by which their destiny and progress are defined. Their physicality becomes the central organizing factor to their future. Physical features, like the nose, hair, mouth, skin, and body contours consciously become the ultimate paradigm to determine the validity of a person. Bad theological anthropology serves as supporting mechanism. Because White is good and Black is bad, what is bad is dangerous and must be eliminated. Therefore, if a human being is Black, he or she is bad, and because he or she is a Black human being, he or she is suspicious.

The effect of this kind of assumption about other human beings is detrimental. The claim that "badness" and criminality are associated with an entire ethnic group as a subconscious and conscious expression manifests itself in several ways. There are two forms of internalizations occurring at the same time. One is the quest to be in control so that what is bad will not take control. The media flood the consciousness of the populace with criminalizing images of the Black man. With no regard for objectivity and truth, one group is presented as "bad" and the other group presented as "good." The "them" against "us" mentality is overtly and covertly displayed daily in the media. Thus, a child grows up, especially a White child, with the mentality that Blacks are criminals. They grow up and are given access to strategic power. With the hatred, suspicion, and negativity introduced into their little innocent minds and memories at such a tender age by the media or by other means, they assume leadership and perpetuate the cycle of hatred, suspicion, and negativity. But they have never had a personal encounter with a Black person except through the media. They went to high school in the suburbs and went to a university or college where Blacks are 0%-5% of the student population. They might not have had a Black friend, or if they did, it was a mere acquaintance. They might never have had a Black instructor or a Black student in either their undergraduate or graduate classes. The consequence is felt immediately when such a person becomes a law enforcement officer. His/her only encounter with a Black person will be as a police officer. You can imagine how he/she might react. Unfortunately, a Black person can become submerged into a terrible race consciousness against other Blacks by association. Racism is a consciousness that is socially constructed and perpetuated.

The other form of internalization is the one concurrently taking place in the mind of the Black person viewed as "bad" because he is Black. He or she internalizes the projections that he/she is Black and, therefore, something must be wrong with him/her. It is true especially for the young person who is often struggling with his/her sense of identity. A healthy family upbringing with positive role models and enforcement might minimize the effects of this internalization. On the other hand, the lack of a healthy family upbringing might enforce the internalized feeling that "I am Black and something is wrong with me." This internalization informs the interpretation of the reality of one's life and the construction and interpretation of meaning for survival. It leads to the distortion of who one is and one's self-image. The only paradigm and lens through which one constructs meaning is a stereotyped paradigm. A stereotyped paradigm consists of a set of negative value systems, externally imposed upon a social group of people. They are racial, tribally, socially, religiously, culturally and politically demeaning. The danger is when a stereotyped paradigm is personalized, that is when I call myself a criminal, a thug, a nigger because society says I am a criminal, a thug, and a nigger.

The internalization of a stereotyped paradigm manifests itself in three ways:

- **Self-distortion:** It manifests itself when one accepts the stereotype that the majority imposes on the minority as its own.
- **Self-deception:** It shows in the conviction that one has internalized this false consciousness to feel safe and secure, even though one does not feel safe and secure.
- **Self-destruction:** It takes place when the internalization of the particular stereotype has come to fruition, and the individual assumes the identity of what he or she negates.

These experience manifest themselves at different levels. They manifest in one's desire to progress and advance despite the odds, while the frustration experienced at having the doors slammed in one's Black face is wearily persistent. It is the agony Black intellectuals encounter when their professional qualifications (or experience) are racially defined in contrast to an emphasis on their accomplishment. It is despair that one experiences when society always says: "You are no good." and "School is not good for you." One must figure out something else to do as despair begins to take over. Despair is when you have come to the "end of your possibilities." In this context, the system, a teacher, or a person in authority with the power to shape and reshape your potential for life has initiated their demise. The structure has seemingly closed the door to your destiny and has opened another one. The frustration and disappointments sometimes manifest themselves through a life of rebellion for many Black students who go through this experience, without much inner strength to persevere and support mechanism.

Commenting on the reasons for the so-called high crime rate among Blacks in 1921, Du Bois argued that the Black individual is perpetually viewed as a criminal with overt or covert suspicion wherever they go. The solution to the elimination of crime, Du Bois wrote, was training, "The chief problem in any community cursed with crime is not the punishment of the criminals but the preventing of the young from being trained to crime" (Du Bois: *The Relation of Negroes to Whites in the South*). The Black person finds him or herself in this circle of racial consciousness, racial stereotypes, freedom, the phenomenon of the color line, poverty, and suspicion Du Bois' emphasis on "training" and "prevention" contrasts Hegel's rejection of any form of rehabilitation for the offender. As an enlightenment figure, Hegel does not positively respond to the consciousness of racism and its sociopolitical and economic influences in the formulation of laws and policies.

He argues that "the criminal act . . . is itself negative so that the punishment is merely the negation of the negation. Actual right is thus the cancellation [*Aufhebung*] of this infringement . . ."[134] Punishment

---

[134] Hegel, PR. 97. "Through a crime, something is altered, and the thing [*Sache*] exists in this alteration; but this existence is the opposite of thing itself, and is to that extent within itself [in sich] null and void. The nullity is [the presumption] that right as right has been cancelled [*aufgehoben*]. For right, as an absolute, cannot be cancelled, so that the expression of crime is within itself null and void, and this nullity is the essence of the effect of crime. But whatever is null and void must manifest itself as such—that is, it must itself appear as vulnerable. The criminal act is not an initial positive occurrence followed by the punishment as its negation, but is itself negative, so that the punishment is merely the negation of the negation. Actual right is thus the cancellation [*Aufhebung*] of this infringement, and it is in this very circumstance that it demonstrates its validity and proves itself as a necessary and mediated existence [*Dasein*]."

is the just cancellation of the criminal act. In this case, deterrence and reform are not relevant since punishment must oppose and cancel the abstract right to commit crime through the will in the concrete world. Punishment must justify the crime within the person since, according to Hegel, "crime in itself is an infinite injury"[135] to the one who commits it. In Hegel, we find a perpetual criminalization of the criminal; the notion that the criminal is an inherent and perpetual one, a stigma he or she must live with for the rest of their lives with little or no hope of escape.

According to Du Bois, the fundamental consciousness in the persecution of crime committed by a Black person is first the "color of the criminal" rather than the crime itself. While he writes about crime and sees the persecution of crime as primarily influenced by the color line, Du Bois is optimistic that the problem of the color line can be resolved in America if both sides of the spectrum recognize the need for change in attitudes and perceptions. As an objective and candid intellectual, Du Bois saw the error on both sides of the spectrum and the need for objective change. For him, the color line, manifested by "proscription and prejudice" undermines "thrifts and intelligence." On the other hand, Blacks, he cautioned, are not to

> Declare that color-prejudice is not the sole cause of their social condition, nor for whites to reply that their social condition is the main cause for prejudice. They both act, as reciprocal, and a change in neither alone will bring the desired effect. Both must change, or neither can improve to any great extent . . . Only by a union of intelligence and sympathy across the color-line in this critical period of the Republic shall justice and right triumph (Du Bois: *The Souls of Black Folk*).[136]

---

[135] Ibid., PR. 218, pg. 251. "Crime in itself is an infinite injury, but as an existence *[Dasein]*, it must be measured in terms of qualitative and quantitative differences and since its existence is essentially determined as a representation *[Vorstellung]* and consciousness of the validity of the laws, its danger is civil society is a determination of its magnitude, or even one of its qualitative determinations."

[136] W.E.B Du Bois, *The Souls of Black Folk* (New York: Dover Publication, INC, 1994), 113.

In summary, the statistics are scary but not hopeless. The existential understanding of the Black community's encounter with God has always been a pivotal source of strength and encouragement. I will now define the above statistics given what the Bible says about prison, the prisoner, and the modern prison system.

Main Points:

- Longer, harsher and mandatory minimum sentences rather than rehabilitation sustain Mass incarceration in the United States' prison system.
- The United States' criminal justice system largely penalizes the "color of the criminal" rather than the crime of the criminal.
- Mass incarceration in the United States is informed by racial stereotypes and the power of the State to criminalize "the other."
- Black men and Black women make up the highest number of those incarcerated in the United States' prison system.
- Mass incarceration has become a Rite of Passage for many Black boys and girls, especially in urban America.

Solution: Adopting a holistic consciousness of humanity and crime will, to a large extent, transform the present paradigm and prism by which we continue to define other human beings about crime and punishment.

"Look, a Negro!' It was an external stimulus that flicked over me as I passed by. I made a tight smile. 'Look, a Negro!' it was true. It amused me. 'Look, a Negro!' The circle was drawing a bit tighter. I made no secret of my amusement. 'Mama, see the Negro! I'm frightened!' Frightened! Frightened! Now they were beginning to be afraid of me. I made up my mind to laugh myself to tears, but laughter had become impossible.
(Frantz Fanon- Black Skin, White Masks, p. 11).

CHAPTER FOUR
Abuse in U.S. Prison and Detention Facilities

The degree of civilization in a society can be judged by entering its prisons.
(Fyodor Dostoevsky).

T he high rates of brutality, suicide, torture, sexual abuse and racism in the United States penal system has blighted its claims for objective justice. In this chapter, we will look at some of the sexual abuses, tortures, and brutalities taking place behind bars, especially against children, and women. [137] Maltreatments in the various prisons, jails, and juvenile detention facilities is perpetrated and instigated by guards on inmates, guards on guards, and inmates on inmates. [138]

Juveniles in Detention

According to the Bureau of Justice Statistics, from 2008-2009 12% of youths in state juvenile facilities and large non-state facilities (3,220 nationwide) were sexually abused with 2.6% (700 nationwide) experiencing sexual abuse from other youths. [139] In

---

[137] http://.www.Therealcostofprison.com
[138] http://jjpl.org/new/
[139] Bureau of Justice Statistics: Special Report: *Sexual Victimization in Juvenile Facilities Reported by Youth*, 2008-2009,http://bjs.ojp.usdoj.gov/content/pub/pdf/svjfry09.pdf
"Between June 2008 and April 2009, BJS completed the first National Survey of Youth in Custody (NSYC) of 166 state-owned or operated facilities and 29 locally or privately operated facilities. The survey, conducted by Westat (Rockville, MD), was restricted to

2010, Reginald Wilkinson, a former director of the Ohio Department of Rehabilitation and Correction reported in an interview with a Justice Department panel that over one in 10 juveniles behind bars under the age of 18 were sexually molested while serving their time in detention. Take for instance the case of Rodney Hulin.

> Rodney Hulin, Jr. [was] handed his first prison sentence at the age of 17 for setting fire to a neighbor's fence. The inexperienced, slight in build, the inmate was repeatedly raped in prison almost immediately upon arrival. He begged authorities to move him to a juvenile facility or otherwise protect him. Despite the fact that his examination by prison doctors verified that Rodney had been raped, he was put back in the general population and essentially told to fend for himself. When he was violated again, Rodney hanged himself in his cell.[140]

When they interrogated Wilkinson about the more than 80% of sexual molestation guards and staff members perpetrated against juveniles, he responded:

> Well, it certainly caught the practitioners off guard as well, in terms of why the excessive numbers in juvenile correctional

---

juvenile confinement facilities that held adjudicated youth for at least 90 days. Facilities were excluded if fewer than 25% of the youth in the facility had been adjudicated, the facility held fewer than 10 adjudicated youth, or if the facility was locally or privately operated and held fewer than 105 youth. All state facilities holding 90 or more youth were included. State facilities with fewer than 90 youth were sampled proportionate to the number of adjudicated youth held, based on the 2006 Census of Juveniles in Residential Placement. Non-state (locally or privately operated) juvenile facilities holding 105 or more youth were initially included, but during the course of the survey, this criterion was increased to 150. At least one facility in each state and the District of Columbia was selected to participate in the survey."

[140] Vincent Schiraldi and Mariam M. Bell: *Prison Rape Is No Joke*, The Washington Post, June 13th 2002, (http://www.vachss.com/help_text/archive/no_joke.html) "Prison rape is no joke. It's a human rights violation of major proportions that needs to be immediately addressed. Because it is counterproductive to return prisoners to society more damaged than when they entered, and because it debases us all to turn a blind eye to anyone's rape, its' time to legislate in this long-neglected arena."

institutions. And actually, the numbers are basically the same, or statistically the same, in adult and juvenile facilities when it refers to inmate-on-inmate's sexual assaults and juvenile-on-juvenile sexual assault. The difference in the juvenile environment is that there are more staff who have improper relationships with juveniles and that makes up the difference between the numbers that we found in adult facilities as opposed to juvenile facilities.[141]

Wilkinson argues that correctional officers and staff members were given background checks and training, but the problem persists. Longer sentences for teenagers make them more vulnerable to abusive guards.

The very individuals that ought to protect and secure their well-being grossly abuse the vulnerability of juveniles in detention facilities. These so-called protectors are the very perpetrators of juveniles' dilemma and destruction in juvenile facilities. Guards and staff members as sexual predators with a history of abusing minors find themselves in uniform with legitimate power and authority. They are protected, given the power, authority, and legitimacy they possess. The international community and human rights groups ought to condemn this behavior. According to Kim Shayo Buchanan,

> In most workplaces, an employee who had sex on the job would be fired. In prison, a report of custodial sexual abuse is more likely to result in punishment or retaliation against the prisoner than in disciplinary consequences for the guard. One might expect the law to furnish incentives for prisons to control such unlawful acts by their employees, as it does for other civil defendants. It does not. Instead, a network of prison law rules-the Prison Litigation Reform Act of 1995 (PLRA), governmental

---

[141] Michel Martin, *Sexual Abuse Persists In Juvenile Detention Centers*, 2010, (http://www.npr.org/templates/story/story.php?storyId=127536419)

immunities, and constitutional deference-work together to confer near-complete immunity against prisoner's claims.[142]

The report raises several questions about the effect and impact of the Prison Rape Elimination Act that was passed in Congress in 2003 concerning the rates of sexual assaults in the United States' prison system.[143]

Most juveniles present in the United States' juvenile detention facilities are Black children. In 2006, there were 11,089 Black teenagers in detention in contrast to 8,167 White teenagers. The detention rate implies that White youth are detained at the rate of 43 per 100,000 while Black youths are detained at the rate of 228 per 100,000.[144] In 2008, the White juveniles' arrest rate dropped to

---

[142] Buchanan, Kim Shayo, Impunity: Sexual Abuse in Women's Prisons, 2007, Pp. 47, (Harvard Civil Rights-Civil Liberties Law Review, Vol. 42) "The misnamed Prison Rape Elimination Act of 2003 does not adequately punish or eliminate sexual abuse. It establishes no sanctions for guards who rape prisoners or for institutions that look the other way when prisoners are raped. Apart from threatening to name prisons that accept federal rape-prevention funds but subsequently fail to comply with as-yet-to-be-adopted national standards, the statute does not take any steps to limit the incidence of sexual abuse in prison. Instead, it establishes procedures for compiling prison rape statistics and allots funds to support prison rape prevention policies. The best that can be said of this legislation is that it at least acknowledges in the congressional findings that prison rape is unconstitutional."

[143] Buchanan, Pp. 70, "The PLRA (Prison Litigation Reform Act) is a status-based law that excludes almost all prisoners claims from the courts. Like historical doctrines designed to deter rape complainants, black witnesses, and married women from bringing white men to court, the PLRA establishes unique hurdles that are nearly impossible for prisoner plaintiffs to overcome. The most damaging hurdle imposed by the PLRA is its grievance exhaustion requirement…[It] requires inmates to exhaust internal prison grievance procedures before they may bring their claims to an outside authority, even if the procedures are complex, inefficient, unfair, or incapable of offering a remedy for the prisoner's claim. If the prisoner has failed to do so, the litigation is dismissed. Thus a prison is virtually insulated from prisoner litigation to the extent that its grievance is brief, and the threat of retaliation deters prisoners from using the process at all. In practice the grievance–exhaustion requirement 'invites technical mistakes resulting in inadvertent non-compliance with the exhaustion requirement, and bars[s] litigant from court because of their ignorance and uncounseled procedural errors. Unreasonably quick grievance deadlines evoke the 'fresh complaint requirement of traditional rape doctrine." Pp. 70.

[144] Brendan Kirby, *Blacks 4 Times More Likely to End Up in Juvenile System,* (http://blog.al.com/live//print.html)

38.89 per 1,000 while Black juvenile arrest rate increased to 453.14 per 1,000. In 2011, Black juveniles were 60% of the juvenile justice population serving life without parole. Accordingly,

> Because of discrimination on the part of the justice system's decision makers, minority youth are more likely to be arrested by police, referred to court intake, held in detention, petitioned for formal processing, adjudicated delinquent, and confined in a secure juvenile facility. Thus, differential actions throughout the justice system may account for minority overrepresentation."[145]

Racially motivated arrests and detentions have become the lot for several Black youths in the United States' juvenile justice system. Juveniles are also given longer sentences for non-violent offenses rather than rehabilitating them. In these detention facilities, they become easy prey for sexual predators masquerading as guards and staff workers. What they cannot do "outside" they now do with legitimate power and authority inside the walls of detention and prison facilities. According to the W. Haywood Burns Institute's December 2008 report:

> In 2004, White youth represented 73 percent of total youth adjudicated delinquent for drug offenses. But they were provided far more opportunities for rehabilitation than Black youth. White youth represented 58 percent of youth sent to out-of-home placement and 75 percent of youth who received probation. In contrast, Black youth represented only 25 percent of total youth adjudicated delinquent for drug offenses. But they represented 40 percent of those sent to out-of-home placement, and a slim 22 percent whose case resulted in probation.[146]

---

[145] *Minority Disproportionality Exists at Various; Decisions Points in the Juvenile Justice System.* (http://www.ncjrs.gov/html/ojjdp/202885/page11.html)

[146] W. Haywood Burns Institute: Adoration of the Question: Reflections on the Failure to Reduce Racial & Ethnic Disparities in the Juvenile Justice System: http://www.burnsinstitute.org/downloads/BI%20Adoration%20of%20the%20Question.pdf

Not only are juveniles in detention subjected to sexual abuse by guards who are paid to protect them, but female inmates are also severely subjected to repeated sexual abuses as they serve their time behind bars.[147]

Female Inmates

The meaning of the twentieth century is the freeing of the individual soul; the soul longest in slavery and still in the most disgusting and indefensible slavery is the soul of the womanhood.
(W. E. B. Du Bois, *The Social Theory of W. E. B. Du Bois, p. 147).*

Between 2008-2009 over 88,500 adult inmates in custody in prisons and jails across the United States were sexually abused at current facilities by guards, staff members, and other inmates. According to the Bureau of Justice Statistics' report: *Sexual Victimization in Prisons and Jails Reported by Inmates, 2008-2009* indicates. Based on a nationwide survey conducted in both state and federal prisons, and jails, 4.4% of inmates in prison and 3.1% of inmates in county jails reported they were sexually molested by both guards and inmates one or more times in the year. The sexual abuse occurred

---

[147] Daniel Lockewood, *Prison Sexual Violence*, (Elsevier, New York, 1980), "Fear is the most commonly mentioned emotion accompanying the target experience. Fear can be a general feeling or a specific apprehension of being physically harmed, sexually assaulted, or killed. Fear can shift from the arena of the incident and it s players to encompass feelings about the entire prison milieu. Fear is intensified by targets' inability to remove themselves from the presence of aggressors easily, and by their propensity to worry about the consequences of aggressive moves. Regardless of the level of force in an incident, fear can be an intense emotion, persisting over time and governing subsequent life-style." Pp. 85

either once or several times. The "*New Federal Report*" writes that sexual abuse plagues the United States' prisons and jails.

> Sexual abuse in detention is a stain on our society,' said Stannow. 'Every day that the Attorney General doesn't finalize the national standards is another day of anguish among prisoner rape survivors, of preventable safety breaches in prisons and jails, and of the significant spending of taxpayers' money on medical treatment, investigations, and litigation that could have been avoided.[148]

In 2004:

- 8, 210 allegations of sexual violence were reported nationwide.
- 42% of allegations involved guards' sexual abuses.
- 37% inmate-on-inmate nonconsensual sexual acts.
- 11% staff sexual harassment; and 10% abusive sexual contact.
- Correctional authorities reported 3.15 allegations of sexual violence per 1,000 inmates held in 2004.[149]

Raped Behind Bars: "Tone Bunton heard the guard coming down the hallway. He wore cheap cologne, and his breath smelled like cigarettes. He scuffed his boots against the floor and opened the door to her cell in Scott Correctional facility, a women's prison in Plymouth Township. 'Come here,' he ordered. The guard pulled Bunton into a bathroom. She wore jogging pants, a T-shirt, and socks. She was the guard's prized possession, a pretty young thing, as he said, 'just the way I like 'em', -short and cute with brown hair, brown eyes, and porcelain skin.' 'Shhh!' he demanded. He yanked down her underwear and pushed her against the sink. 'No' she screamed in her head. 'No, please, no!' But she was scared to death,

---

[148] Business Wire: *New Federal Report: Sexual Abuse Plagues U.S. Prisons and Jails, 2010* (http://www.businesswire.com/news/home/20100826005772 /en/Federal,)

[149] Insideprison.com, *Prison Rape: The Challenge of Prevention and Enforcement, 2006,* (http://www.insideprison.com/prison-rape.asp,)

and the words wouldn't come out. 'I'm choking, please, stop, I'm going to die,' she thought. And he raped her. Bunton said nothing. It would become the theme of her life, a way to survive the next 16 years in prison. When he was done, he stepped back. 'Shhh!' he said, with his finger to his lips. He smiled and left. Bunton stood there, numb, her pants at her ankles. She Was 19."[150]

Pregnant Behind Bars: "I am 7 Months pregnant [and] I got pregnant here during a sexual assault. I have been sexually assaulted here numerous times! The jailers here are the ones doing it.'"[151]

The below incident indicates that women, who do not initially enter prison pregnant can leave the prison pregnant or have been pregnant before their release. Since no other male works with the females except the guards, the evidence points to them as the culprits. Furthermore, there is the issue of the treatment of pregnant inmates. The treatment of pregnant women in the United States' prison system deserves a thorough investigation.

Christopher Hitchens writes in his article: *The Scandalous Brutality of U.S. Prisons* in 2005:

> If a female prisoner becomes pregnant, therefore, you can be reasonably certain that something is, or has been, going on...You may have been nauseated by pictures of women soldiers humiliating Iraqi males in Abu Ghraib, but there are jails in this country where male officers are not prevented from supervising female inmates, in the showers and in the lavatories, and making whatever comment or gestures they feel like making. This kind of thing just doesn't happen in comparable countries, where there are conjugal visits, inspections, and openness to drop-bys from human-rights organizations.[152]

---

[150] Jeff Seidel, MI: *Sexual Abuse of Women Went Unheeded-2 of 5 articles and Human Rights Watch Report. 2009.* (http://realcostofprisons.org/blog/archives/2009/01/mi_ab)

[151] Nicole Summer, *Powerless in Prison: Sexual Abuse Against Incarcerated Women, 2007,* (http://www.rhrealitycheck.org/print/5597.)

[152] Christopher Hitchens, *The Scandalous Brutality of U.S. Prisons.* In Vanity Fair, 2005 (http://www.vanityfair.com/politics/features/2005/09hitchens200,

The United States' prison system has seen an enormous increase in female incarceration over the decades because of the war on drugs. Also, the criminalization of trauma and addiction for women, mothers, and pregnant women have also contributed to the increasing rates of females' incarceration. According to Buchanan,

> Since the advent of the war on drugs, imprisonment of women has increased even faster than the imprisonment of men. Between 1986 and 2004, the number of women in prison for all crimes increased 400%, while the number of African American women in prison increased 800%. Between 1986 and 1996, the number of women serving time in state prisons for drug crimes increased 888%, compared to 522% for men. The war on drugs has racially targeted African America women and Latinas as it has their male counterparts; in New York State, 82% of Latinas and 65% of black women sentenced to prison were convicted of drug crimes, compared to 40% of white women.[153]

Correctional facilities across the country have not adequately responded to the increase in females, mothers, and pregnant women incarcerated in their facilities. Apart from the sexual abuses perpetrated by guards and staff members, little has been done to address the problem of incarcerating pregnant women and mothers. Women are facing high rates of incarcerated in the United States' prison system, especially for non-violent drug offenses. Per the National Women's Law Center,

> There are now more women behind bars than at any other point in U.S history. Women have borne a disproportionate burden of

---

[153] Buchanan, Kim Shayo, *Impunity: Sexual Abuse in Women's Prisons, 2007*, Pp. 52-53, "After conviction, black women and Latinas are likely to be sentenced to prisons, while white women are likely to be released. Department of Justice figures reveal that white women constitute only 29% to 36% of American women in federal, state, and local prisons, while more than two-thirds of incarcerated women are black or Latina. By contrast, white women make up a substantial majority-62%-of women released on probation. These statistics suggest either that many white women are being tried and convicted for minor crimes that do not warrant imprisonment, or that they are being imprisoned because they are white." Pp. 54

the war on drugs, resulting in a monumental increase of women who are facing incarceration for the first time, overwhelmingly for non-violent offenses. This rampant incarceration has a devastating impact on families. Most of these women, unseen and largely forgotten, are mothers. Unfortunately, pregnant women, incarcerated women, and their children are subject to federal and state correctional policies that fail to recognize their distinct needs or honor their families.[154]

The report below and statistics adopted from the National Women's Law Center should better clarify this contradiction and predicament in the United States' prison system in the 21st century.[155]

Report on Shackling

History will have to record that the greatest tragedy of this period of social transition was not the strident clamor of the bad people, but the appalling silence of the good people.
(Martin Luther King, Jr.).

The Restraining of Pregnant Women in U.S. Prisons:

The United States incarcerates pregnant women, and some women get pregnant during incarceration. The treatment accorded pregnant women in the United States' prison system regardless of the crime committed is abysmal. Pregnant women are shackled during pregnancy and delivery with an increase in the number of pregnant inmates. Incarceration of pregnant women implies the

---

[154] National Women's Law Center, (The Rebecca Project For Human Rights) 2010, Mothers Behind Bars: A State-by-state report card and analysis of federal policies on conditions of confinement for pregnant and parenting women and the effect on their children.
[155] National Women's Law Center:

criminalization and demoralization of the pregnant woman, the pregnancy, and the baby.

> A shackle…is a U-shaped piece of metal secured with a clevis pin or bolt across the opening or a hinged metal loop secured with a quick-release locking pin mechanism. They are used as a connecting link in all manner of rigging systems, from boats and ships to industrial crane rigging. A shackle is also the similarly shaped piece of metal used with a locking mechanism in padlocks.[156]

Based on the above definition, shackling is the process of padlocking the feet of a pregnant woman, but especially padlocking her hands and feet to the bed during delivery. This lack of respect for women during their most vulnerable moment and condoned in the American criminal justice system reflects a great decline in the respect for human dignity in the American social consciousness.[157] This is a travesty.

The National Women's Law Center 2010 report titled: *Mothers Behind Bars* provides some troubling conclusions regarding State and Federal correctional facilities across the country as to how they treat pregnant women and mothers behind bars. Following are sections of the report that relate specifically to the care of pregnant women in U.S. prisons and jails:

> **"Overall grades:** Averaging the grades for prenatal care, shackling…family-based treatment as an alternative to incarceration: twenty-one states received either a D or F, both of which are considered failing grades. Twenty-two states received a grade of C, and seven received a B. The highest overall grade of A was earned by one State-Pennsylvania.

---

156 Wikipedia: http://en.wikipedia.org/wiki/Shackle
157 NPR: Difficult Births: Laboring and Delivering in Shackles.
http://www.npr.org/templates/story/story.php?storyId=128563037

Prenatal care: Thirty-eight states received failing grades (D/F) for their failure to institute adequate policies or any policy at all, requiring that incarcerated pregnant women receive adequate prenatal care, even though many women in prison have higher-risk pregnancies:

- Forty-three states do not require a medical examination as a component of prenatal care. Forty-one states do not require prenatal nutrition counseling or the provision of appropriate nutrition to incarcerated pregnant women.
- Thirty-four states do not require screening and treatment for women with high-risk pregnancies.
- Forty-eight states do not offer pregnant women screening for HIV. – Forty-five states do not offer pregnant women advice on activity levels and safety during their pregnancies.
- Forty-four states do not make advance arrangements for deliveries with hospitals.
- Forty-nine states fail to report all incarcerated women's pregnancies and their outcomes.

Shackling: Thirty-six states received failing grades (D/F) for their failure to comprehensively limit, or limit at all, the use of restraints on pregnant women during transportation, labor and delivery, and postpartum recuperation.

- Twenty-two states either have no policy at all addressing when restraints can be used on pregnant women or have a policy, which allows for the use of dangerous leg irons or waist chains.
- When a pregnant woman is placed in restraints for security reasons, eleven states either allow any officer to make the determination or do not have a policy on who determines whether the woman is a security risk.

- Thirty-one states do not require input from medical staff when determining whether restraints will be used.
- Twenty-four states do not require training for individuals handling and transporting incarcerated persons needing medical care or those dealing with pregnant women, specifically, or have any policy on training.
- Thirty-one states do not have a policy that holds institutions accountable for shackling pregnant women without adequate justification.
- Thirty-four states do not require each incident involving the use of restraints to be reported or reviewed by an independent body.

Family-Based Treatment as an Alternative to Incarceration: Seventeen states received a failing grade (F) for their lack of adequate access to family-based treatment programs for non-violent women who are parenting.

- Seventeen states have no family-based treatment programs, while thirty-four states make such programs available.
- Of the thirty-four states with family-based treatment programs, thirty-two offered women the option to be sentenced to these programs in lieu of prison, while two did not.

Prison Nurseries: Thirty-eight states received a failing grade (D/F) for failing to offer prison nurseries to new mothers who are incarcerated. While a far less preferred option than alternative sentencing, prison nursery programs still provide some opportunity for mother-child bonding and attachment.

- Thirty-eight states do not offer any prison nursery programs.
- Of the thirteen states that do offer such programs, only two allow children to stay past the age of two.

74

- Three of the thirteen programs offer therapeutic services for both mother and child."[158]

The children of incarcerated pregnant mothers are often put into the foster care system. The guards that impregnate the women are also not identified. Their children are aborted, imprisoned with the mothers, or shipped to foster homes. Incarcerated mothers most often do not have parental rights over their children. Guards abuse female inmates with no remorse or moral compunction. Unfortunately, their female victims are left to bear the existential scars, longing, and weeping for the children they have brought into this world, but cannot handle and nurture in their arms, or the children they were forced to abort.[159]

"No one in a civilized society is sentenced to be raped and assaulted in prison."[160] It is time to enact legislation that bans the incarceration of pregnant women on both State and Federal levels. Alternative sentencing should be developed specifically for

---

[158] National Women's Law Center: "Early in 2009, 22-year-old Joan Laurel Small was an inmate of Collier County Jail located in Naples, Florida. Small complained for nearly two weeks that she was leaking amniotic fluid, but was ignored by Prison Health Services. The fetus died when its skull collapsed while in utero. The prison also failed to promptly arrange to have the fetus removed from Small, placing her at risk for infection, infertility and even death. This incident exposed a whole host [of] alarming health conditions for women imprisoned at the Collier County Jail: inmates shackled to hospital beds during labor; a pregnant woman with gestational diabetes going weeks without testing and treatment; and an inmate forced to deliver in a prison drop-off area after law enforcement ignored the woman's complaints of labor contraction for hours. The American Civil Liberties Union of Florida has requested that Collier County Jail disclose how many inmates hare reported miscarriages and stillborn babies as well as the facility's policies for pregnant inmates." Pp. 28

[159] Buchanan, "The rules that construct prison law impunity are designed to shield correctional authorities from the trouble and expense of litigating an anticipated flood of groundless prisoner litigation. The reach of these rules is not limited to sexual violence. They also vitiate the state's duty to protect prisoners against myriad other equally serious abuses that occur in men's and women's prisons... The abusers are government actors, and their action cannot be excused as the overzealous but good-faith pursuit of any legitimate penological objective. Sexual abuse is well known to be severely underreported, both inside and outside prison.

[160] Jeff Seidel: http://realcostofprisons.org/blog/archives/2009/01/mi_sexual_ab

pregnant women. I believe pregnant women should not be incarcerated at most given a limited sentence.

A letter from an inmate to Stop Prisoners' Rape:

A rumor had spread through the facility that I was pregnant. I'm not sure how the rumor got started, but medical staff came to my cell and forced me to provide a urine sample that they could use to test for pregnancy. They did not ask me any questions, offer me any support, or seem at all concerned for my well-being. That same night, three guards, two females and one male, came into my cell, sprayed me in the face with mace, handcuffed me behind my back, threw me down on the ground, and said, 'We hear you are pregnant by one of ours and we're gonna make sure you abort.' The two female guards began to kick me as the male guard stood watch. The beating lasted about a minute, but it felt like ten or more. Afterward, the male officer uncuffed me and they left.[161]

Female inmates were afraid to speak out for fear of being dismissed as liars and targets of abuse. Female prisoners are convicts as well. In justifying their actions, guards have argued that convicted felons will lie to get back at the system. Thurs, for years, female inmates endured the brunt of the guards' sexual maltreatment. Fear of retaliation from guards, shame, and embarrassment are often the price incarcerated women pay when they report their abuses. Human rights groups began reporting rampant sexual abuses in US prisons in the 1990s as normal occurrences.

The fear of brutal retaliatory methods perpetrated by correctional officers compounds the humiliation, insecurity, and

---

[161] Nicole Summer, 2007, *Powerless in Prison: Sexual Abuse Against Incarcerated Women.* http://www.rhrealitycheck.org/print/5597

stigma associated with sexual maltreatments endured behind bars.[162] Calls are monitored so calling a hotline for help does not often work in the victim's favor. Confidentiality in prison with a therapist is nonexistent. It is a closed system, and the victims know they will face retaliation.

> In 1986, a correction officer at Crane, Raymond Raby, was dismissed after admitting during a police interview that he had sexual relations on a nightly basis with different women incarcerated at Crane. Raby's exploits came to light after a prisoner, Jackie K., reported that Raby molested her. According to Jackie K.'s statement, Raby entered her cell at night and woke her up. He took her into a visiting room where he grabbed her and kissed her, then fondled her breast.... Shortly after Jackie K. complained about him, another prisoner reported seeing an officer fitting Raby's description having oral intercourse with a third prisoner.[163]

The raping of Bunton together with more than 500 women went uninvestigated in the 1990s at several prisons in Michigan. 18 women were brave enough to come forward to sue The Michigan Department of Corrections for $50 million under a class–action lawsuit. According to an Ann Arbor civil rights lawyer: Several of the women complained of different kinds of molestations to which guards had subjected them. Some of the women reported in their trial testimonies that: "Guards ran their hands over the women's legs, buttocks, and breast under the guise of security. When it

---

[162] Nicole Summer, 2997, "Despite the widespread underreporting, some statistics exist. First, there are about 200,000 women incarcerated in the U.S (in federal, state, local and immigration detention settings), a number that is growing exponentially and that makes up about 10 percent of the total prison population. Amnesty International reports that in 2004, a total of 2,298 allegations of staff sexual misconduct against both male and female inmates were made and more than half of these cases involved women as victims, a much higher percentage than the 10 percent that women comprise of the total prison population. It can vary from institution to institution, but in the worst prison facilities, one in four female inmates are sexually abused in prison, stay Stannow."

[163] Jeff Seidel,

became clear the guards wouldn't be punished, some grew so brazen that they fondled women in front of other inmates and guards, or openly masturbated in the prison yard."[164]

The power dynamic evident in these abuses is obvious. The use of legitimate power to abuse and molest implies in several ways the abuse of that power and authority. The inmates are in a disadvantaged position while the guards are in an advantaged position. Rape and trade for sex are often means of acquiring some basic things.[165] It is illegal in the United States for guards to have sexual contact with an inmate, regardless.

Another area of sexual abuse not often talked about is the rampant nature of male sexual abuse. The spread of HIV/AIDS and other forms of chronic and debilitating diseases have helped to shine a light on this area in the United States' prison system.

He who passively accepts evil is as much involved in it as he who helps to perpetrate it. He who accepts evil without protesting against it is really cooperating with it.
(Martin Luther King, Jr.).

Male Inmates

Christopher Marshall argues that more men are raped behind bars than women on the outside. In prisons, they do not often use condoms

---

[164] Jeff Seidel,

[165] Buchanan, Kim Shayo, Pp. 56, "When prison fail to enforce prohibitions on sex between guards and prisoners, they create considerable pressure on women who do not cooperate with guards' sexual demands. '[I]t is not only actual physical and verbal sexual abuse but also the potential for this abuse that makes it so powerful a form of control over women inmates.' So-called protection from other predatory guards, for example, would be a meaningless incentive if sexual contact between guards and prisoners allows guards to coerce sex through material inducements that are strikingly petty. One Framingham prisoner was given a piece of contraband bubblegum by flirtatious guard, only to find out he expected sex in return. She realized, belatedly, that 'she might just have sold herself for a piece of gum.'"

According to the Human Rights Watch 2000-2001 report of three years of research, guard-on-inmate, and male prisoner-on-prisoner sexual abuse in the United States is very high regardless of race or ethnicity. Rape takes place in prison every day. The anguish associated with this experience is enormous, as evident in this account from the Human Rights Watch:

> A Florida prisoner whom we will identify only as P. R. was beaten, suffered a serious eye injury, and assaulted by an inmate armed with a knife, all due to his refusal to submit to anal sex. After six months of repeated threats and attacks by other inmates, at the end of his emotional endurance, he tried to commit suicide by slashing his wrists with a razor. In a letter to Human Rights Watch, he chronicled his unsuccessful efforts to induce prison authorities to protect him from abuse. Summing up these experiences, he wrote: 'The opposite of compassion is not hatred, it's indifference.'[166]

When an inmate is sexually abused, he "becomes entrapped in a sexually subordinate role." Prisoners refer to the initial rape as "turning out." The victim's identity is redefined. He has been proven to be weak, vulnerable, and "female" in the eyes of other inmates. Regaining his "manhood" and the respect of other prisoners can be extremely difficult.[167] He is considered a "punk" or "turn out" and vulnerable to continuous sexual exploitation, especially from the first perpetrator or perpetrators who often claim the role of protecting the victim from other inmates. The victim essentially becomes the property of the first perpetrator. According to Human Rights Watch, victims of prison rape, in the most extreme cases, are the slaves of the perpetrators. Forced to satisfy another man's sexual appetites whenever he demands, they may also be responsible for washing his clothes, massaging his back, cooking his food, cleaning his cell, and myriad other chores. They are frequently "rented out" for sex, sold, or even auctioned off to other inmates, replicating the

---

[166] Human Rights Watch: http://www.hrw.org/reports/2001/prison/report.html
[167] Ibid.,

financial aspects of traditional slavery. Their most basic choices, like how to dress and whom to talk to, may be controlled by the person who "owns" them. A female one may replace his name. Like all forms of slavery, these situations are the most degrading and dehumanizing experiences a person can experience.[168]

The stigma of becoming the sexual property and slave of another inmate spreads from prison to prison. It is worse for the victim if sentenced to several years of imprisonment since he could be transferred to other prisons. Per the Federal Bureau of Prisons Report, "approximately 9-20% of prison inmates are targets of aggressive sex acts during their incarceration. Several independent studies, however, place the percentage of homosexual rape significantly higher than this official calculation. Rape is one of the most serious safety issues in lockups, jails, and prison settings."[169]

According to Human Rights Watch, once a prisoner is sexually violated, they are marked during their entire imprisonment. This analysis provides an understanding regarding the link between mass incarceration of Black men and the HIV/AIDS epidemic in the Black community. Black men are over 42% of the prison population of the United States. Blacks are only 13% of the total United States population. In the United States' prison system, the use of condoms is not a policy, and it is not encouraged.

I saw the tears of the oppressed and they have no comforter; power was on the side of their oppressors…If you see the poor oppressed in a district, and justice and rights denied, do not be surprised at such things; for one official is eyed by a higher one, and over them, both are others higher still.
(Ecclesiastes 4:1, 5:8).

---

[168] Ibid.,
[169] (http://beyond-the-illusion. com/files/issues/condom.txt).

Suicide and Death

Based on the Boston Globe,

> Suicide, the single leading cause of death in local jails, accounted for 29 percent of all jail deaths between 2000 and 2007, according to a July report released by the Bureau of Justice Statistics of the US Department of Justice. A total; of 8,110 inmates died in custody of local jails in the seven-year period.[170]

Massachusetts' has the highest inmate suicide rate in the United States. The rate of suicide in Massachusetts' correctional facilities is four times that of the national average. In 2010, there were eight reported suicides in the Massachusetts Department of Corrections. According to the Criminal Justice website report on suicide in 2010;

> Suicide is the leading cause of death inside U.S prisons. Nationwide, about 16 of every 100,000 prisoners take their lives every year. But this year, Massachusetts is experiencing a rash of suicides that has driven that number to 71 per 100,000 and that's just so far. With five months left in the year, that rate is bound to get higher.[171]

The death and suicide reports announced to the public are often not the formal reports. Non-suicide-related death news is not brought to the public's awareness unless reported. Death by

---

[170] Shelley Murphy, MA: *Another Suicide Raises Questions About Safety of MA Prisoners*, August 16th 2010, the Boston Globe
(http://realcostofprisons.org/blog/archives/2010/08/ma_another_s)

[171] Criminal Justice, (http://criminaljustice.change.org/blog/view/why_massasachusetts_h)
According to an investigation report, "Prisoners on suicide watch these last few years (in Massachusetts) have been placed in empty cells, made to wear gowns instead of regular prison garb and their visiting privileges have been revoked. They have been deprived of belonging like books, mail and photos."

HIV/AIDS and other diseases including tuberculosis, syphilis, etc., have caused untold numbers of death in the United States' prison system. While the suicide rates have escalated, guards' brutalities and inmate on inmate brutalities have also increased the number of deaths in the United States' prison system. Human Rights Watch and other organizations have argued over the years that annual death rates in the United States prison system are extremely high, considering the high rates of sexual abuses, brutalities and inhumane retaliatory methods, especially those perpetrated by guards on inmates.

The range of brutality, including solitary confinement inflicted on inmates causes psychosocial destabilization, mental illness, feminization of the male inmate, prostitution, depression, and suicide and death in the prison environment.

Similarly, the increasing news of the death of immigrants detained in the United States' detention facilities should raise some concerns. For instance, the case of Guido R. Newbrough who died on Nov. 27, 2009, in an ICE jail in Virginia from bacteria of the heart valves (Endocarditis), which could have easily been cured by giving him antibiotics. According to the report:

> His family and fellow detainees say the infection went untreated, despite his mounting pleas for medical care in the 10 days before his death. Instead, after his calls for help grew insistent, detainees said guards at the Piedmont Regional Jail in Farmville, Va., threw him to the floor, dragged him away as he cried out in pain, and locked him in an isolation cell...Dr. Homer D. Venters, an expert in detention care, who learned about the case from Mr. Newbrough's family and reviewed the autopsy, said available evidence showed violations of detention standards that let the detainee's treatable local infections rage out of control. Dr. Venters, a public health fellow at New York University, was critical of the medical care in immigration detention when he testified last year at a

Congressional subcommittee hearing, and in an Immigration and Customs Enforcement advisory group.[172]

Between January 2004 and November 2007, there were 66 deaths of immigrants reported in detention facilities in the United States' immigration custody. Death of immigrants in detention facilities does not often reach the deceased's relatives as quickly as one would expect. It is difficult for families to get adequate redress regarding the death of their relatives in immigration facilities across the United States. For example, quite often, detainees who die in immigration facilities that are run by private prison corporations.[173]

According to Stephen Lendman in his article: *Torture in US Prisons*, written in 2010,

> Two deaths were in Phoenix, AR county jail, run by 'America's Toughest Sheriff, Joe Arpaio." He writes, "You don't want to be fettered in one of Sheriff Joe's jails." His toughness often ends tragically. In one tape, nine deputies manhandled Charles Agster, a tiny man, a mentally disturbed drug user, arrested for

---

[172] The Real Cost of Prison, "Accounts of Mr. Newbrough's last days echo other cases of deaths in immigration custody, including one at the same jail in December 2006, which prompted a review by immigration officials that found the medical unit so lacking that they concluded, 'Detainee health care is in jeopardy.'... But Immigration and Customs Enforcement never released those findings, even when asked about allegations of neglect in that death, of Abdoulai Sall, 50, a Guinea-born mechanic with no criminal record whose kidneys failed over several weeks, instead, official defended care in that case and other deaths as Congress and the news media questioned medical practices in the patchwork of county jails, private prisons and federal detention centers under contract to hold noncitizens while the government tries to deport them." http://realcostofprisons.org/blog/archives/2009/01/va_death_in

[173] Nina Bernstein: *CCA Detention Centers: For Immigrants Who Died in U.S. Custody, Few Details Provided.* "Federal official say deaths are viewed internally by Immigration and Customs Enforcement, which reports them to its inspector general and decides which ones warrant investigation. Officials say they notify the detainee's next of kin or consulate, and report the death to local medical authorities,; who may conduct autopsies...But critics, including many in Congress, say this piecemeal process leaves too much to the agency's discretion, allowing some death to be swept under the rug while potential witnesses are transferred or deported. They say it also obscures underlying complaints about medical care, abusive conditions or inadequate suicide prevention." http://realcostofprisons.org/blog/archives/2008/05f/cca_detentio

disturbing the peace. Restrained in a chair, one deputy knelt on his stomach, 'pushing his head forward onto his knees and pulling his arms back to strap his wrist to the chair. Bending someone double for any length of time' can cause 'positional asphyxia...After 15 minutes, he's unconscious. He's already brain dead. Hospitalized he expired three days later... Another tape showed guards severely beating a man, Scott Norberg, including Tasering him 19 times and forcing him into a restraint chair. He suffocated...Other inmates suffered abuse, including beating causing broken bones, a broken neck, and internal injuries. One man died from septicemia (blood poisoning) after a month in a coma.[174]

Reports of death and abuses are very difficult to retrieve and track from private prison corporations across the country. Access to the records of prisoners in private prisons around the nation is not often available to the public. It perpetuates the high rate of abuse and maltreatment of inmates and detainees in private prisons and immigration detention facilities.[175]

---

[174] Lendman, Stephen, *Torture In US Prisons, 2010*, (http://www.rense.com/general92/TORTURE.HTM) Bureau of Justice Statistics Special Report: Suicide and Homicide in State Prisons and Local Jails. 2005, by Christopher J. Mumola.

[175] Price, pages, 48-49, (http://wwws.flpba.org). "For example, in 1995 in Elizabeth, New Jersey, at the privately operated Immigration and Naturalization Service (INS) detention center for illegal aliens, prisoners were abused by underpaid, inadequately trained guards where under contract with the for-profit firm Esmor Correctional Services (now known as Correctional Services Corporation). Guards at this facility had to endure a riot that involved 300 prisoners. Twenty illegal immigrants were injured during the riot. In addition, the detainees seized control of the building to voice their opposition to being mistreated; they demolished the interior of the building and held two guards hostage for five hours before police managed to quell the riot. The INS launched an investigation to determine the reasons for the riot, and their investigation found that Esmor official failed to exercise control over their guards, who were found to be improperly trained or had not been fully investigated before hired by Esmor...Private prisons have yet to prove that they are more effective in managing prisons."

Racism Behind Bars

***The persons, then, who come forward in the dawn of the 20th
century to help in the ruling of men must come with the firm
conviction that no nation, race, or sex, has a monopoly of
ability or ideas; that no human group is so small as to deserve
to be ignored as a part, and as an integral and respected part,
of the mass of men; that, above all, no group of twelve million
black folk, even though they are at the physical mercy of a
hundred million white majority, can be deprived of a voice in
their government and of the right to self-development without
a blow at the very foundations of all democracy and all
human uplift.***
(W. E. B. Du Bois. *Of the Ruling of Men*, Published in 1920 in
Darkwater).

Another poignant, but often unpublicized area of abuse in the United States' prison system is guards-on-guards and guards-on-inmates racism. Correctional officers are over 65% White across the United States. In most states and county facilities, the number is over 80%. [176] The United States' correctional workforce is a predominantly White male conclave and over 80% of prisons and jails are constructed in rural and suburban White communities. On the other hand, over 60% of those incarcerated in the United States' prison system are Black and Hispanic men, women and juveniles taken from urban America.

Based on the sociopolitical and economic history of the United States, racial conflicts and allegations of racism cannot be far-fetched. Also, increased racial hatred behind prison bars in rural

---

[176] Correctional Officers Facts: http://www.realpolice.net/forums/department-corrections-142/75271-correctional-officers-facts.html

85

America cannot be dismissed[177] as a "consequence of the increasing dependence of rural communities on prisons."[178] Several authors and former corrections officers have researched and documented the level of blatant organized racist practices in prisons, especially in rural areas across America.[179] According to Huling

> Individual acts of racism in prisons include the wearing of Klan-style robes or hoods at work and the wearing or displaying of Confederates for skinhead flags or insignias by employees inside prisons. The problem becomes one of organized or organizational racism when excuses like 'hey, it was just a joke,' or 'that's my heritage' are accepted and translated by prison management as 'white boys will be white boys.'[180]

---

[177] White Prison Gang Task Force: Aryan Brothers: "Aryan Brotherhood members make up less than one percent of the nation's prison inmate population, yet the white prison gang is responsible for 18% of all prison murders."
http://whiteprisongangs.blogspot.com/2009/05/aryan-brotherhood.html

[178] Huling, Pp. 6-7 "In 2000, the Washington Department of Corrections paid $250, 000 in an out-of-court settlement to black officers who had accused it of condoning racist behavior at the Clellam Bay Corrections Center located in a remote northwest corner of the state, where most of the prison guards are white, formerly unemployed loggers… 'The people we work without there are exloggers,' said former guard Doris Washington, a plaintiff in the Clellam Bay suite. 'They have never come in contact with the outside world per se. they don't know how to deal with us because they've never been around us.' Though Clellam Bay's prisoner population is 48 percent minority, only 4 of its 326 employees are black. The lawsuit states that black officers were denied promotions, subject to threats and racial epithets like 'coon,' and that minority prisoners were harassed and set up for beatings. Some white guards had taken to calling Martin Luther King Jr. Day 'Happy Nigger Day' and a handful of guards openly bragged about association with hate groups like the Ku Klux Klan. A similar lawsuit filed in 1999 by black employees of Washington Correctional Center in Shelton, also included complaints about organized neo-Nazi activities including 'Hail Hitler' salutes among some whiter officers and distribution of hate literature inside the prison."

[179] Huling, Pp. 6.

[180] Huling, Pp. 6 (Kelsey Kauffman, The Brotherhood: Racism and Intimidation Among Prison Staff at the Indiana Correctional Facility-=Putnamville, Russell Compton Center for Peace and Justice, DePauw University, April 2000. Kelsey Kauffman, 'Confronting White Supremacy Among Prison Employees.' Speech given at National Conference of the National Association of Blacks in Criminal Justice, July 23, 2001, Cincinnati, Ohio.): "In at least six states guards have appeared in mock Klan attire in recent years. Guards have also been accused of raced-based threats, beatings and shooting in 10 states. Lawsuits have been filed in at least 13 states by black guards alleging racist harassment or violence from

Locked Up and Locked Down: Multitude Linkers in Limbo

The prison environment engenders racial tension with White correctional officers caught perpetrating racial slurs and actions against Black and Hispanic inmates. According to the Southern Poverty Law Center's 2000 Intelligence Report:

> When unruly inmates in Texas created a disturbance in their fourth-floor cellblock, they surely expected some sort of reprimand. Bruce Parker, a supervisor at Houston's Harris County Jail, delivered one they wouldn't soon forget. Calling the prisoners "niggers," Parker allegedly went on to threaten them with violence. He announced to his charges that he was "down with the KKK," and had been a Ku Klux Klan member, in fact, since the age of 25. Parker, who was fired following the July incident, isn't the only corrections officer who invoked the Klan or white supremacist ideology to teach inmates—and sometimes other guards and even wardens — who's boss. In at least six states, guards have appeared in mock Klan attire in recent years, and guards have been accused of race-based threats, beatings, and even shootings in 10 states. In addition, suits have been filed in at least 13 states by black guards alleging racist harassment or violence from their own colleagues.[181]

Racism among prison guards is not only perpetrated against inmates but fellow guards as well. Several Black and Hispanic correctional officers have reported racial abuses at the hands of White correctional officers. In his article: *NAACP, 46 Prison guards claim*

---

white colleagues. And uncounted settlements have been reached in civil filed by guards or inmates, where damages are sealed by court order. The Florida NAACP has joined more than a hundred black employees in filing suit against the state Department of Corrections for harboring and condoning overt racism in the state's prisons. Black officers and prisoners have accused white officers of carrying so called 'nigger knots' (small knotted nooses on their key chains worn as symbols of solidarity); of wearing and display9ing racist symbols (such as Klan tattoos) at work; of routinely using racist epithets; and of retaliating against employees-black and white-who challenge these practices."

[181] Southern Poverty Law Center: *Allegation of Racist Guards are Plaguing the Correction Industry.* http://www.splcenter.org/get-informed/intelligence-report/browse-all-issues/2000/fall/behind-the-wire

harassment, racism, retaliation published in the St. Petersburg Times, Adam Smith writes:

> African-American prison officers who claim rampant racism in Florida's prison system say the Department of Corrections is retaliating against them through intimidation and life-threatening harassment. The allegations, made in a series of federal court filings in recent days, spurred a group of state lawmakers to embark on an "emergency" fact-finding tour of several north Florida prisons Tuesday night... The NAACP and 46 black officers from throughout Florida are suing the prison system in federal court, claiming it systematically blocks promotions for African-American staffers and subjects them to work in environments that include everything from racial slurs to lousy shift assignments to "KKK" graffiti.[182]

Lawyers have often appealed to the Eighth Amendment to the United States Constitution, which prohibits terrible and inhumane punishment to derive some form of protection against the sexual abuses and molestations described here. The Fourth Amendment enhances the Eighth Amendment which also protects and guarantees the individual's right to privacy and individual integrity. It has been applied to protect female inmates from "search stripping" in the presence of prison guards, intrusive pat-frisking and unusual and intrusive forms of visual surveillance, often by the lower courts.[183] According to Jeff Seidel:

> Constitutional protections of prisoners' rights are enforceable via lawsuit filed by or on behalf of prisoners, or by the U. S. Department of Justice (DOJ). Historically, U.S. prisoners have achieved most of their landmark prison victories through private litigation, particularly by suits litigated by prisoner's rights groups such as the National Prison Project of the American Civil

---

[182] St. Petersburg Times: *NAACP, 46 Prison Guards Claim Harassment, Racism, Retaliation.* http://www.sptimes.com/News/041801/State/NAACP__46_prison_guar.shtml
[183] Jeff Seidel, MI: *Sexual Abuse of Women Went Unheeded*-2 of 5 articles and Human Rights Watch Report.

Liberties Union or the National Prison Project of the National Women's Law Center. However, if certain stringent intent requirements are met, the DOJ may criminally prosecute abusive prison officials under federal civil rights provisions. In addition, the DOJ has the statutory right to investigate and institute civil actions under the Civil Rights of Institutionalized Persons Act (CRIPA) whenever it finds that a state facility engages in a pattern or practice of subjecting prisoners to 'egregious or flagrant conditions' in violation of the constitution.[184]

The prisoner's rights are also protected under international laws and human rights treaties to which the United States is a signatory. The most important international laws that protect prisoners in the United States' prison system include *The International Covenant on Civil and Political Rights* (ICCPR) which the United States ratified in 1993. The law is the Convention against Torture and Other Cruel, Inhuman or Degrading Treatment or Punishment that the United States also ratified in 1994.[185] The above laws have been interpreted by several authoritative bodies to include sexual abuse, especially considering the rampant nature of sexual abuses and degradation evident in the United States' prison system.[186]

---

184 Jeff Seidel: MI: *Sexual Abuse of Women Went Unheeded*-2 of 5 articles and Human Rights Watch Report.

185 Buchanan, . "In states that have not criminalized all sexual contact between guards and prisoners, even sexual touching and quid pro quo sexual exploitation short of rape may not be clearly unlawful. Qualified immunity may particularly impeded allegations of institutional failure to investigate sexual abuse, as it is not clear how cursory an investigation must be before it will be found clearly unlawful. The usual justifications for the application of qualified immunity to government actors do not fit the context of civil claims for custodial sexual abuse. First, an important justification for the qualified immunity rule is to avoid 'unwarranted timidity,' or the fear that 'government officials who are exposed to money damages for the full costs of their constitutional violations will become overly cautious or quiescent, reducing their activity to suboptimal levels and shying away from socially beneficial risks.' This concern is irrelevant within the context of sexual contact between prisoners and guards, as there is no optimal level of custodial sex which the threat of liability might over deter."

186 Jeff Seidel: "To constitute torture, an act must cause severe physical or mental suffering and must be committed for a purpose such as obtaining information from the victim,

In 1995, seven female prisoners who narrated several instances of horrible sexual abuses by guards and staff member sued the Michigan Department of Corrections (MDOC). Human Rights Watch personnel who followed the case up to the United States Department of Justice investigated the abuse. The allegations included every form of sexual assault, sexual abuse, sexual harassment and sexually oriented surveillance methods implemented in the women's correctional facilities. Under the criminal code of Michigan, the sexual maltreatment of the female inmates should have amounted to a misdemeanor.[187]

---

punishing her, intimidating her, coercing her, or for any reason based on discrimination of any kind. Cruel, inhuman or degrading treatment or punishment includes acts causing a lesser degree of suffering that need not be committed for a particular purpose. The ICCPR guarantees the prisoners' right to privacy, except when limitations on this right are demonstrably necessary to maintain prison security. When prison staff members use force, the threat of force, or other means of coercion to compel a prisoner to engage in sexual intercourse, their acts constitutes rape and, therefore, is torture. Torture also occurs when prison staffs use force or coercion to engage in sexual touching of prisoners where such acts cause serious physical or mental suffering. Instances of sexual touching or of sexual intercourse that does not amount to rape may constitute torture or cruel or inhuman treatment, depending on the level of physical or mental suffering involved. Other forms of sexual misconduct, such as inappropriate pat or strip searches or verbal harassment, that do not rise to the level of torture or of cruel or inhuman treatment, may be condemned as degrading treatment."

[187] Jeff Seidel, MI: *Sexual Abuse of Women Went Unheeded*-2 of 5 articles and Human Rights Watch Report. (http://realcostofprisons.org/blog/archives/2009/01mi_sexual_ab,) "Under Michigan's criminal code, any sexual touching with a prisoner by an employee of or a volunteer with MDOC constitutes fourth-degree 'criminal sexual conduct,' a misdemeanor. (665) The provision was added in 1988 to a pre-existing section of the criminal code that outlawed sexual touching with someone between the ages of thirteen and sixteen who is physically or mentally incapacitated or that is accompanied by force of coercion. The law applies to sexual contact irrespective of a prisoner's alleged consent. Given the position of authority held by a corrections employer over a prisoner, the Michigan legislature found 'the usual notions of consent do not apply.' The MDOC employees manual reiterates that prohibition on sexual contact with a prisoner and informs employees that such conduct constitutes a crime under Michigan law. Under certain circumstances, corrections officers who engage in sexual intercourse with prisoners may be charged with third or first degree criminal sexual conduct. Third degree criminal sexual conduct occurs when an individual uses force or coercion to have sex. First degree sexual conduct applies to intercourse that occurs under specified aggravating circumstances.... MDOC continued noncompliance led the Sixth Circuit Court of Appeals, in 1991, to issue a stern rebuke to the department and to uphold the

Main Points:

The American prison system is littered with sexual abuse, torture, brutality, suicide, and human rights violations.

- Correctional officers inflict a high percentage of abuse of inmates in U.S. prisons.
- Abuses by correctional officers often go uninvestigated.
- The United States has the highest rate of incarceration of pregnant women, mothers, and women in the world.
- Pregnant women in U.S. prisons are shackled during pregnancy, during birth, and after birth.
- Babies born to pregnant women in prisons are often put into foster homes.
- Close to 80% of the U.S correctional system workforce are White men.
- Racism perpetrated by White guards is rampant in U.S. prisons with Black and Hispanic men accounting for over 60% of the U.S prison population.
- Guards-on-inmates and inmates-on-inmate abuses are rampant in the United States prison system.

It is not right, my fellow-countrymen, you who know very well all the crimes committed in our name, it's not at all right that you do not breathe a word about them to anyone, not even to your own soul, for fear of having to stand in judgment of yourself.
(Jean-Paul Sartre: *The Wretched of the Earth*).

---

appointment of a special administrator, a remedy the Circuit Court once found overly intrusive. The Sixth Circuit concluded: [The] history of this case shows a consistent and persistent pattern of obfuscation, hyper-technical objections, delay, and litigation by exhaustion on the part of the defendants to avoid compliance with the letter and spirit of the district court's order. The plaintiff class has struggled for eleven years to achieve the simple objectives of equal protection under the law generally, and equality of opportunity specifically... The Sixth Circuit's rebuke did not appreciably affect MDOC's recalcitrance, and women have continued to face difficulties gaining the remedies ordered by the court."

AN ANALYTICAL DISCUSSION

CHAPTER FIVE
The Bible, Prison, and Freedom

Whoever sets any bounds for the reconstructive power of the religious life over the social relations and institutions of men, to that extent denies the faith of the Master.
(Walter Rauschenbusch).

This analysis looks at Dr. Christopher Marshall's work on prison and the Bible. He argues that the Bible rejects imprisonment, condemns the modern prison system, does not condone the criminal as an inherent criminal, and does not condone the racialization of crime or prisoners.

According to Marshall, the United States and New Zealand topped the chart for the highest number of people imprisoned in 2002. The Washington Post-*New High In U.S. Prison Numbers* reports that

> With more than 2.3 million people behind bars, the United States leads the world in both the number and percentage of residents it incarcerates, leaving far-more-populous China a distant second, according to a study by the nonpartisan Pew Center on the States.[188]

More jails, more money spent, more stringent measures, more people behind bars, and more association of crime with Black men. In the King James Version of the Bible, prison appears ninety times, prisoner thirteen times, and prisoners twenty times. Marshall asserts

---

[188] Dr. Christopher D. Marshall, *Prison, Prisoners and the Bible* (A paper delivered to "Breaking Down the Walls Conference," Tukua Nga Here Kia Marama Ai, Matamata, 14-16 June, 2002 [Accessed. Feb. 2, 2009) p. 1.

that most church folks don't want to know what is happening in the prisons and the consequences of more imprisonment. They are happy that "criminals" are locked up. Once they are out of sight, they must be out of mind. According to Marshall, that is the problem. The Bible is about justice and not injustice, repentance and not reproach, rebuke and not hostility, forgiveness and not exclusion, restoration and not destruction.

He argues that the prison system today is a recent development in human history because prisons before the eighteenth century were non-institutional. According to Marshall, "prisons have served principally as holding tanks, where offenders could be detained before trial or to the carrying out of the sentence of the court, such as execution, exile or enslavement, or until debts or fines, had been paid." [189] There are, however, exceptions in the Bible. The Babylonians imprisoned King Jehoiachin for thirty-seven years in Babylon (2 Kings 24:15, 25:2-7; Jer. 52:31-34). King Jehoahaz died in an Egyptian prison; not much is found on King Zedekiah after he was captured and jailed by the Babylonians (2 Kings 25:2-7; Jer. 39:1-7, 52:3-11).

In its initial development, the modern prison system was viewed as a face-lift, a center for reshaping, reforming, rehabilitating, and eventually restoring the individual to the society in contrast to the old system. The old system in its treatment of prisoners was humiliating. What was intended to change the brutal system of torture and bodily harm became a penal system of punishing the soul and the body in prison.[190] This new system, with good intentions, was initiated by the Church he notes.

---

[189] Ibid., 3.

[190] Ibid., 3 "Prior to this time, the system of punishment was largely arbitrary and often brutal. There was little proportionate gradation of penalties. The sanction imposed upon offenders depended largely on the whim of the magistrate or prince, and there was a much stronger emphasis on hurting the body, by torture, mutilation, the stocks or the gallows, than on reforming the mind or changing the character of the offender. But as the idea of rehabilitation took hold, it contributed considerably to mitigating the severity of criminal law. The function of imprisonment changed from being a system for detaining people before sentence to becoming a mode of punishment in its own right."

What began as a humanitarian gesture has since become one of the most violent and inhumane institutions in modern society. Twice as many rapes, for example, take place inside US prison as are inflicted on women outside of prison. Caging people for long periods of time, depriving them of autonomy and responsibility and self-respect, tearing apart their families, so that the innocent relatives and children of inmates suffer, throwing together dysfunctional and damaged people into a huge zoo, and all in [the] name of 'correcting' them, is both inhumane and counter-productive . . . Nor is it a response to crime that can claim any biblical support whatsoever.[191]

Imprisonment was not a strange phenomenon to most of the individuals in the Bible. From the Old Testament to the New Testament, we see biblical characters going in and out of prison for various reasons. Joseph was sold into slavery and subsequently imprisoned on false accusations. Samson and Daniel were imprisoned for political reasons; the prophets were imprisoned for religious reasons; and finally, Peter, Paul, and other disciples were imprisoned for causing religious and social upheaval wherever they went with the preaching of the resurrected Christ.[192] For Paul, while at one time he was the one locking people up; after his conversion, he became a jailbird and was constantly locked up. For example, in Philippi, Caesarea, and Rome, [193] so that he could take on the name "prisoner of Jesus Christ."[194] Perhaps that was the identity on the record for Paul. According to Marshall,

Prison is not the only criminal sanction cited in the New Testament. A whole variety of other judicial and extra-judicial punishments are also mentioned in passing, decapitation, drowning, hanging, precipitation, mutilation, stoning, excommunication, exile, chaining, putting in stock, scourging,

---

[191] Ibid., 4.
[192] Acts 8:3, 9:1-2; 22:4-5; 26:10; Phil. 3:6.
[193] Acts 16:19-40, 23:10ff; 24:27; 28:16, 20, 30.
[194] Eph. 3:1; Philem. 1, 9, cf. 2.Tim 1:8.

sawing in two, torture (which came in many forms), and crucifixion. Quite often, the victims of such barbarities are not evildoers but those at the margins of mainstream Jewish and Greco-Roman society.[195]

The leaders of the first church had a recidivism rate that was high. But it was the gruesomeness of imprisonment, its impact on one's freedom and sense of personhood that on several occasions demanded God's intervention. Marshall gives five reasons for imprisonment in biblical times:

First: "Imprisonment was a cause of great suffering." [196] For example, Jeremiah was dropped in a "cistern" and "dungeon where he remained for a long time" for prophesying that Jerusalem would go into captivity. He suffered greatly and, upon being released, begged not to be sent there again.[197]

The prophet Micaiah was imprisoned and punished with starvation on a diet of just bread and water. [198] Prisons were associated with death, starvation, torture, suicide, etc.[199]

Second: "Imprisonment in biblical times was viewed as 'an instrument of oppression more than an instrument of justice.'"[200] There is one place where the prison is considered a "judicial

---

[195] Christopher D Marshall, Beyond Retribution: A New Testament Vision for Justice, Crime and Punishment (Michigan, William B. Eerdmans Publishing Company 2001) P. 16 n.

[196] Marshall Prison, *Prisoners and the Bible*, 4.

[197] Jer. 38, 37.

[198] I Kings 22:27; 2 Chron. 18:26.

[199] Marshall, *Prison, Prisoners and the Bible* "The psalmist speaks of 'prisoners in misery and in irons,' captives who 'groan' and are 'doomed to die.' Job considers Shell to be preferable to imprisonment, for at least there 'the prisoners are at ease together [and] do not hear the voice of the taskmasters.' Things were no better in New Testament times. With few exceptions, prisons in the Roman period were dark, disease-ridden, and overcrowded places. It was common for prisoners to die in custody, either from disease or starvation, brutal torture, execution, or suicide. Imprisonment is commonly described by ancient authors as a fate worse than death; even the thought of it was appalling." (Ps. 107:10, 79:11; 102:20; Job 3:18; Matt. 25:36; Matt. 18:34; Heb. 13:3; cf. Jer. 52:11; 2Chron. 16:10; Mark 6:14-29; Phil. 1:19-24).

[200] Marshall, *Prison, Prisoners and the Bible*, P. 7.

sanction" for unlawful behavior, and in this case, it was the refusal to abide by the king's decree and the law of God in the book of Ezra.[201] Marshall argues that "prison is not prescribed as a criminal sanction in the Old Testament Law." Israel subsequently introduced it.[202]

Israel introduced prisons because of the "development of standing armies and military establishments"[203] Restitution, instead of retribution and imprisonment, were considered adequate means of dealing with offenders. The goal of imprisonment was "expressing repentance toward God." [204] Furthermore, the communal nature of Israel's social life made it difficult for wrongful actions to be considered independent individual actions. This idea was based on the belief that the consequences of individual's actions affected the entire community.[205] Furthermore, Israel's experience of slavery in Egypt did not allow prisons and imprisonment to be God-approved forms of punishment. As a solution, God told Moses to set aside six cities as "Cities of Refuge" for offenders. For Marshall,

> Israel's experience of imprisonment in Egypt made an indelible mark on her national memory, and consequently on her social policy. Israel never forgot the bitterness of slavery, nor God's action of setting her free from servitude. Israel therefore never used enslavement as a form of criminal punishment. She did still practice a form of slavery, but never felt easy doing so, and the covenant law built into the institution had several limitations and humanitarian protections. Indeed, in many ways Hebrew slavery was a more humane institution than modern imprisonment, for

---

[201] Ezra 7:26.
[202] Marshall, *Prison, Prisoners and the Bible*, P. 7.
[203] Ibid., 7.
[204] Ibid., 7.
[205] Ibid., 7.

slaves were at least permitted to participate in normal family and community life.[206]

Long-term imprisonment instead was used for political and military purposes; for example, individuals of defeated armies and their leaders, disloyal leaders of the governing authorities, those captured for enslavement, prisoners of war, and religious leaders as a result of religious persecution.[207] While imprisonment was used to punish political dissidents, criminals, religious opposition, etc., the modern form of imprisonment has added two new dimensions: economic profitability and racial sentencing enforced by a racial criminalization of Black men. The biblical analysis of prisoners and imprisonment does not mention an economic industry built on prisoners, neither a form of imprisonment and sentencing influenced and informed by racism. Per Marshall,

> Scriptures' consistently negative perspectives on imprisonment should alert us to the inherent tendency of all prison systems to oppress and abuse people in the name of some higher goal. This, in turn, should caution us against excessive or normative reliance on imprisonment as a means of dealing with wrongdoing, since the power to imprison can so easily become a mechanism of oppression.[208]

He goes on to argue that criminal justice cannot be devoid of social justice when those easily imprisoned are the economically poor, marginalized, victims of discrimination, deprived, and disadvantaged in the society. The tendency to sentence individuals to longer prison terms takes the focus from "the real causes of crime which has much to do with social circumstances as with individual wickedness." [209] Marshall argues that the Bible's idea of

---

[206] Ibid., 8.

[207] Ibid., 8.

[208] Ibid., 8.

[209] Ibid., 9. "Under certain social conditions people will turn to crime that in other social climates would remain law-abiding. Poverty, unemployment, racial inequality, social

imprisonment is different from that of the modern prison industry. He writes, "The criminal justice system can oppress as well as protect; it can persecute as well as punish. Once again, the alertness of the biblical tradition to this fact should caution against a naive trust in the capacity of the cage to conquer sin."[210]

Third: The Bible identifies imprisonment in with "the spirit and power of death."[211] Prisons connote death, alienation, separation, and estrangement. Prisoners acquire new criminal behaviors in prison, and old ones often enhanced as first-term offenders are lumped together with hardened criminals. Marshall argues that "plain common sense should tell us that we will never defeat violence by throwing nonviolent people together within a violent environment, especially in light of what has been called 'the contagious nature of criminality."[212] Imprisonment is often a source of anxiety, meaninglessness, and hatred. The biblical solution, which reveals the mind of God, seeks to liberate the prisoner by "setting the captive free, opening prison doors."[213]

Fourth: Marshall argues that "God wants to set prisoners free." The Bible does not endorse imprisonment. It views imprisonment as a

---

prejudice, family dysfunction, and drug and alcohol abuse all have a role in fostering crime. A significant proportion of criminal offenders have been offended against as children before they become offenders. It is crucial rather than being content to divide individuals into categories of guilty and innocent and tossing the guilty into jail. Society's own complicity in the creation of criminals is quickly lost sight of in the outpouring of moral indignation at individual offenders. It is also important to recognize that the law which criminals break is not a neutral transcription of absolute morality. It is an irrefutable fact, Barbara Hudson insists, that the law is predominantly reflective of the standpoint of the powerful, property-owning, white male and that the justice system bears down more heavily on the poor and disadvantaged than on the rich and the powerful. One recent study in New Zealand shows how the government puts far more money and resources into cracking down on welfare benefit fraud than on white collar crime, even though the cost of white collar crime and corporate fraud is up to 10 times higher than the cost of all other crimes combined."

[210] Ibid., 10.
[211] Ibid., 10.
[212] Ibid., 10.
[213] Ibid., 11.

tool of injustice, oppression, and the spirit of death. Prison is viewed negatively in the Bible and only serves as an opportunity for God's divine deliverance. Marshall argues that this negative evaluation of prison provides a premise for God as the one who wants to set the captive free and to break the chains of bondage. The psalmist speaks of a God who "looks down from his holy height, from heaven . . . to hear the groans of the prisoners, to set free those who were doomed to die." The same God who "made heaven and earth, the sea, and all that is in them," the same God who "executes justice for the oppressed [and] gives food to the hungry" is also the God who "set the prisoners free."[214]

In Luke 4:16-20, Jesus, Marshall argues, was not simply interested in spiritual and psychological liberation but liberation from "material structures and ideological systems which robbed [humans] of freedom and dignity."[215] Freedom, in the biblical sense, according to Marshall, has "both external and internal dimensions."[216] The Old Testament defines freedom as liberation from "external constraints (poverty, debt, slavery, oppression, and military oppression)." The New Testament, on the other hand, emphasizes an "interior moral and spiritual freedom that the Christian gospel brings, a freedom from demons and despair, from sin and selfishness, from guilt and greed."[217]

One can, therefore, argue that the biblical notion of freedom is holistic and contradicts the modern form of imprisonment and "vengeful Penology" as Muelder argues. The underlining reason for the Bible's opposition to the modern form of imprisonment and the penal system is that it categorically undermines God's holistic plan and purpose for the human being. There is no biblical justification for imprisonment based on race and the profit margin.

---

[214] Ibid. 11 Deut. 7:8; 24:18; Ps. 68:6, 79: 11; 102:10-16; 118:5; 146:7; Isa. 427; 45:13; 49:13; 49:8-9; 61:1; Micah 6:4; Zech. 9:11; Acts 5:19; 16:25-26; 1Pet. 3:19; Rev. 2:10, Ps. 102: 19, cf. 79:11, 146: 6-7
[215] Ibid., 12.
[216] Ibid., 12.
[217] Ibid., 12.

This holistic understanding of freedom as being pivotal to Jesus' ministry is evident in the Gospels. Salvation in this regard does not only cater to the spiritual and interior estrangement of the human being, but to the individual's external and psychosocial estrangement in the concrete realm of human sociopolitical and economic activities. It is with this mindset that we can only understand and be sensitive to the prevailing rates of incarceration and detention of Black men. To reiterate, the Bible does not mention or hint at a racial motive for incarcerating prisoners, neither do we find any argument for prisons and detention facilities as industrial complexes for economic gains in the Bible. According to Marshall, even if these forms of imprisonment and sentencing practices were present, they would fall under the category of human oppression, thus necessitating God's divine intervention and deliverance. Marshall's analysis also raises another point of contention: our perception of the other person and how we relate to him/her. As evident in the analysis, racial and criminalizing assumptions as instruments of justice undermine the nature of justice and lead to an ontological distortion of the human being. It is in this context that we can adequately understand the debilitating feeling of racially informed and influenced detention and incarceration as they generate questions concerning the worth and inherent dignity of their victims.

> *To crush underfoot all prisoners in the land, to deny a man his rights before the Most High, to deprive a man of justice-would not the Lord see such things?*
> (Lamentations 3:34-36).

I conclude this section with the testimony of Brother Steve Johnson. I met Steve at Morning Star Baptist Church in Boston and knew that there was a transformative moment in his life. Steve's conversion experience captures the ethos of this work in several ways: once a criminal is not always a criminal. The human being can be rehabilitated, restored and reintegrated into society as a viable member.

Main points:
- Mass incarceration in the United States undermines divine justice, fairness, and equality.
- The biblical model pursues liberation for the poor, the oppressed and the marginalized.
- The American penal system undermines God's holistic plan for justice, redemption, rehabilitation, and restoration.

Turn upon yourself and be fine
Turn upon yourself and be refined
Turn upon yourself and be defined
Turn upon yourself and be affirmed
The you that is fine is the you refined
For the you that you find is you affirmed
Since you defined is you that is fine
Turn upon yourself and be fine
(George Walters-Sleyon)

Stevee Johnson:
"My Story from Gangster to God"

I was born in a small town called Nashville in Georgia, outside of Atlanta. I had three brothers and four sisters. We were a family with issues.

I saw my father constantly beat my mother for over twenty-five years. Because of this, most of my brothers and sisters moved away from home early at the ages of fifteen and sixteen. I was the baby, and I had to stay home and witness everybody leaving. Around the age of six or seven, I witnessed my father continue to

102

beat my mother as usual. On one occasion, when my father was beating our mother, my oldest brother went to help my mother. He began to beat my father. My father ran into the house to get his 12-gauge shotgun and shot my brother Robert in the leg. Back in the '60s and '70s, the EMTs were slow. When my brother finally made it to the hospital, his leg was amputated, but he ended up bleeding to death.

Because of this experience, I lost all sense of emotion. Hatred grew in my heart. I began to hate both men and women. I eventually began to hate people. With this, I began to grow up very mad and angry as I continued to watch my father get drunk and beat my mother every weekend. I began to hate the weekends because I knew my father would be getting drunk and subsequently beat my mother. This impacted my upbringing as I grew up with lots of hatred and a bad temper, which I also transferred into my schooling.

At school, I was always fighting since I didn't have peace in my home. Unfortunately, we never went to church. I grew up having no clue about who Jesus Christ is. As I grew older, my only thought was to get some money and leave my home area. At the age of fourteen, I caught my first aggravated assault charge. Because of my temper, I was sent immediately to a boy's correctional facility. I did approximately two years there. But at the facility, other young men with the same issues, no real father and no clue about Jesus also surrounded me. Unfortunately, we learned more evil ways from one another than anything good, and furthermore, no one came to visit me for two years. I was released on the sixth month before my sixteenth birthday. At this point in my life, I had become strong headed and would not listen to anyone.

At sixteen, I stole my first motorcycle. I was caught and sent back into lockup. I got out on my eighteenth birthday. While in jail, I learned the art of selling drugs. Still no one mentioned Jesus Christ to me, and furthermore, my family didn't attend church. At this point, my life was quickly turning for the worst and out of control. At eighteen, I was in my first high-speed chase and standoff with the police. Between the drug charges, possession of guns and money, I was given seven years in the State's prison system. I had never been locked up like that before in my entire life.

While in prison, I became even more violent because my experience from my previous imprisonment taught me that, in prison, you must earn your respect. I learned how to beat people down in prison. On my first day of entering the State Prison, as I entered my bunk and tried to relax, one of the prisoners, who was also notoriously known, came to claim me. We entered a fight. The police guards came, and in the process of separating us, they hit me terribly at the back of my head, and blood began to ooze out. I became unconscious and fainted. I was given thirty-two stitches while in lockup. Thinking about it, I should have sued the police for treating me as such, but I was ignorant of my rights, and I had a bad temper. It was in self-defense because the underlining culture was that he came to try me to see if he could subdue me.

I did three years in prison and paroled out at twenty-one. With no better education and career or family to return to, while on parole, I ended up hustling and selling drugs, robbing people, and had no clue as to what it meant to be a man. I had not heard about Jesus Christ, and no one from the church even approached me to share the gospel. So, from twenty-one onward, I sold drugs, slept with several women, from city to city. I went from Miami to Cleveland, Ohio, from New York to Atlanta, and back to Miami. I kept on trafficking cocaine from Miami to Atlanta to Jacksonville, Florida. My clientele included blacks and whites, people in business, lawyers, professionals, nonprofessionals, hustlers, addicts, and pimps. Because of my business and business connections, I came to own several cars, my own house yet with no peace of mind, no love, and no future.

At this point in my life, I was sniffing cocaine and gambling. In1991, I was shot in my left arm from a drive-by shooting. But my life was spared, and yet I could not turn to God. I became even more of a gangster and worse in my pursuit. However, something happened that made me lose everything that I had. I came to the end of my life, and I was hopeless. I found myself homeless in Atlanta with my two daughters and reduced to nothing. I was troubled.

It was then that I could hear from God. I began to repent to God, but I didn't know that I was repenting. I was only asking God if he would raise me up and make me the man that he wants me to be, I will never turn away from the gospel. When I said that, I had no clue as to what I was saying, but instantly peace came into my heart and I had such a burning desire to know this God of the Bible.

From August 18 of 1996 to this day, God has changed my life, has blessed my soul, and has given me a charge to keep. So I must tell the world that Jesus Christ saves no matter who you are and where you have been. The gospel of Jesus Christ is for every woman, man, child, whomsoever. Yes, I may have a CORI, but I also have a conscience; I may have a record, but I also have redemption, my mess became my message. Now I work with teenage boys to help point them to truth and righteousness.

*   *   *

Steve is now a pastor with a ministry in Atlanta, Georgia. He goes around preaching the Word of God. He completed his GED and got some formal training in working with young people and has worked with the Department of Youth Services in the Boston area.

What it means to be a human person, who Jesus Christ is 'for us', and the relationship between faith and ethical responsibility are, as intimated, interconnected. So it is that the Church which presupposes the sociality of humanity and is brought into being and sustained by the vicarious action of Christ, exists vicariously in the world, that is, for the sake of the 'other'. This means that the Church exists for the sake of restoring justice, reconciliation and peace.
(John W. de Gruchy - *Reconciliation: Restoring Justice* p. 93).

CHAPTER SIX
Am I Worthy as I Am?

It's a feeling of despisal, A feeling of rejection
It's a feeling of not being a part
Of the whole
It's a feeling of the other
A feeling of distortion
It's a feeling of a disconnect
Of the soul
    Am I worthy as I am?
    Am I worthy ask I Lord
    Am I worthy as a person?
Should be taken as they are
You see the staring of the eyes
The hasting of the footsteps
You see the distance that is made
Because of you
It's a struggle for acceptance
A struggle to participate
A struggle to accommodate
You and I
    Am I worthy as I am?
    Am I worthy ask I Lord
    Am I worthy as a person?
Should be taken as they are
Why should I feel this way?
Why should I feel this way?
This stereotype feeling
This stereotype guilt on my mind
    Can anybody help me?
    Can anybody tell me?
    Can anybody hear me cry?
    The anguish of rejection
    Why . . . ? Why . . . ? Why . . . ?

(George Walters-Sleyon)

In this chapter, I provide a theological interpretation of the person based on three conceptual understandings. (1) Pope John Paul with a contemporary view of human beings as created in the image of God. (2) St. Augustine's notion of self-certainty and one's awareness of self as a human being. (3) W. E. B. Du Bois' existential understanding of personhood in a social context of racial construction. I argue that one's theology and their views of human beings are not mutually exclusive but mutually inclusive. In that light, the possibility of ontological distortion can be a prevailing experience for an individual or group of individuals as victims of negative theological and anthropological perceptions.

I define ontological distortion as any treatment that negates and reduces the inherent worth of a person. It is that which defines a person strictly on material and physical grounds. It undermines and reduces the essential nature of a person to what is secondary. Racially motivated arrests, sentencing, and mass incarceration lead to ontological distortion of self because it is racially and economically motivated. A racialized form of ontological distortion forces the racialized person to consistently question their sense of selfhood because of society's stigmatization of their humanity.

They constantly inquire: *Where did I come from?* (Sense of origin)*, Who am I?* (Sense of identity), *What is wrong with me?* (Sense of alienation), *Why am I here?* (Sense of meaning), and *Where am I going?* (Sense of destiny). These questions speak of hopelessness and meaninglessness characterized by alienation and agony. Reflecting on the conflict within about identity and self-worth, Dr. King, Jr. warns that:

> The Negro must be grasped by a new realization of his dignity and worth. He must stand up amid a system that still oppresses him and develop an unassailable and

majestic sense of his own value. He must no longer be ashamed of being black. [218]

Over 2.2 million individuals in their cells and over 7.2 million individuals caught in the American correctional system across the US struggle with their sense of worth and identity. Those in detention for deportation are baffled by the lack of explanation for their lack of release or deportation. Those in prisons are baffled by the relationship between the trivialization of who they are in the sentencing process and the crime they have committed or didn't commit-violent or non-violent. The Black detainee and the Black prisoner have a shared experience: their African origin and Blackness, the stereotype associated with their Blackness and the criminalization of their Blackness. Both have forfeited their freedom, and with the prevailing statistics highlighting the frequency with which they are arrested, detained, and incarcerated, both share an inescapable fate: racialization, criminalization, and mass incarceration.

In this chapter, I also theologically analyze the consciousness that criminalizes and the assumptions associated with the racialized form of incarceration. Any view that promotes the consciousness of essential superiority of one group of people and the essential inferiority of another group of people based on race, color and physicality invariably seek to develop and promote a theological consciousness consistent with that view. A racialized theological understanding develops and promotes a racialized anthropology. A racialized theology produces a racialized perception of other human beings. An individual's theology influences his/her anthropology, i.e., one's consciousness of God influences one's consciousness of humanity. If theology reflects the way in which we have experienced God and the understanding and knowledge derived from that experience is used to inform our social relationships and practices, then our anthropology or how we perceive other human beings is highly influenced and informed by our theology. If not,

---

[218] King, 1968, p. 41.

then we are deliberately implementing a strange dichotomy or divide between our theology and how we perceive others to avoid accountability and live in denial.

The situation of mass incarceration and human abuse in the United States' prison system should concern us holistically as human beings. The situation deserves a theological understanding because it affects us as human beings, not only physical beings but ontological beings threatened by the experience of nonbeing. The threat of "Nonbeing" implies the devaluation of a human being. Nonbeing in its nature is that which militates against being. This devaluation says to the human beings, "You are an object"; and because you are an object, you are devoid of feelings, reactions as a normal human being, responses, and other forms of attributes associated with "real" human beings. Mass incarceration in America objectifies human beings for commercial reasons.

The threat of nonbeing expresses itself subtly or overtly in the form of racial depersonalization. It feels like living on the fringes or the fence, always a part of the whole but never becoming a member of the whole. A member of the whole exists with the assurance of accommodation by other members of the whole, as an equal who is worthy of contributions and benefits, as a participant in the structural and institutional makeup of the whole, expected of every member. This wholeness is informed by a sense of acceptance by the whole and protected from other members of the whole who may threaten the membership of others.

Living as such for the Black person is felt interiorly and exteriorly in the world. It is interior in the sense that it affects the existence of the individual, a people, a community, and a group. The experience is theological in the sense that knowledge of the total reliance on the God of one's being is sought in the struggle against the threatening use of race, skin color, hair texture, physical contours, spelling, and sound of one's name, etc. They serve as the sole lens through which the construction of policies and meaning occurs, and realities are interpreted. The effect for the Black person, upon experiencing the sense of negation, is felt beyond the physicality of who he/she is, in the inner sanctum of their being. The one who sees only the deemed and material reflection of skin color and all forms of physicality either consciously knows he/she is inflicting pain or is subconsciously acting on impulses buried in the storehouse of one's memory: the interior part of one's being.

The effect of ontological distortion is directed at the "essence" of the person. In the case of a Black person, their Blackness is perceived as socially pathological and, therefore, must be discouraged in certain respects. It is considered a negation and, therefore, must be resisted. The worst fear in this social milieu for a non-Black person is to wake up in the morning, look in the mirror and realize they are Black and his or her hair has turned "kinky," commensurate with a Black body. At this, they might scream, "I am doomed, and beauty is doomed." On the reverse, a Black person who wakes up in the morning and discovers that he or she is transformed into a White person might think, "I have arrived." But why should we think like this? Is it not because of what Blackness has come to symbolize and what Black people are made to represent while Whiteness and lightness have come to symbolize wealth, status, beauty, privilege, etc.?

We are afraid to become what we have created because we see the consequences of what we have made, and it is threatening to us. Blackness is devalued and Black human beings, criminalized. We have psychologically conditioned our minds to think that any being other than us is an inferior being, and we cannot be reduced to the status of inferior beings because inferiority connotes criminality. Because of this socio-psychological conditioning of our minds, we have redefined and reduced the "image of God," an ontological nature in every human being to a domesticated category. The reduction of human beings to "things" and manipulative racial categories for sociopolitical and economic advancement distort what God has made good. This distortion, historically experienced in the United States and manifested in the present rate of incarceration of Blacks in the United States is extremely harmful. Its effects are felt daily in the corridors of academia; the confines of media rooms, in the place of public policy formulation, in the courtrooms and boardrooms of economic institutions where life-defining decisions are developed.

We are conscious of the fact that the use of the knowledge of God to assert our superiority is inconsistent with the nature of God, but we perpetuate and condone it because of the sociopolitical and economic benefits and privileges it accrues for us. It is a sin, but we must tolerate it. We do not want to talk about it because it will convict us. We'd rather not talk about it because conviction often leads to transformation and accountability. We do not want to be confronted with the inconsistency of what we believe about the knowledge and nature of God and what we practice. We live a life of cognitive dissonance and are quite okay with it. A racial anthropology is a result of a racialized theology. Why should a group of people languish in prison, their families destroyed, their men, women, and boys given distorted and twisted images about themselves while their wives, mothers, husbands, fathers, and children weep for them? Where is the shared sense of human feeling, empathy, and identification? Racism has hardened the heart of the United States as she refuses to feel the pain and see the scars of its racialized victims. The United States does not want to be accountable, but deep in her consciousness, she knows such pain and scars exist, some caused, some influenced, and some self-inflicted.

The distortion of the image of God in the victims of mass incarceration in the United States' prison system and its perpetuation through structural and institutional abuse deserve a theological investigation. This distortion has accrued sociopolitical and economic privileges for some and their descendants. In contrast, it has systemically allowed the deprivation of human rights for others and their descendants while subjecting them to a life of generational impoverishment.

This ontological devaluation of other human beings complicates the notion of estrangement for the racially marginalized. As human beings collectively estranged from God, the racially marginalized feel the second sense of estrangement. This estrangement is felt in their social encounters. The racially marginalized person not only feels the burden of this ontological distortion of self but also consistently endures the distortion of self in their concrete social world. They face the struggle of often overcoming this subject/object distinction of self. This "twoness (duality)" of the self: How they perceive themselves as subjects with feelings, emotions, needs, wants, desires, ambitions, aspirations, and dreams often contradict how the outside world, the sociopolitical milieu, and others, perceive them as objects.

Racism has established the prism through which others are perceived. Racial perceptions create conditions in which the identity, aspirations, and dreams of the racialized are easily abandoned leaving them to weep on the inside. Often, they do not know that they are weeping because they have become accustomed to their painful existence. The reality of the pain is shown in their sighing, their longing to be free of the burden of stigmatization and unnecessary stereotypes. They weep not with tears in their eyes, but with tears on the plates of their hearts and the walls of their souls. They have wept so much, and since no one hears them, they have become one with their tears. When you see them, you feel them; when you hear them, you know them; when they sing, the pain is expressed in the melodies of their songs, the beat of their rhythm, and the tempo of their music. They are weeping, but only the one who seeks to understand the shared mutuality of human connectedness will feel the pulsating beats of tears dropping gently in latent agony. King captures this existential experience beautifully when he writes about *The Dilemma of Negro American*. He explains:

> The central quality in the Negro's life is pain-pain so old and so deep that it shows in almost every moment of his existence. It emerges in the cheerlessness of his sorrow songs, in the melancholy of his blues and in the pathos of his sermons. The Negro while laughing sheds invisible tears that no hand can wipe away.[219]

---

[219] King, 1968, p. 103.

For King, being a Black man or woman is a dialectical existence of pain and peace, tears, and laughter, suffering, and survival often without a climax or synthesis. He writes:

> Just as the ambivalence of white Americans grows out of their oppressor status, the predicament of Negro Americans grows out of their oppressed status. It is impossible for white Americans to grasp the depths and dimensions of the Negro's dilemma without understanding what it means to be a Negro in America.[220]

Blacks in the United States he argues have felt the pain of "persistent denial" and rejection based on the color of their skin. With Black humanity reduced to Blackness and the socio-cultural and economic assumptions manufactured against Blackness, their humanity goes through the constant fluctuation of acceptance and rejection, suspicions and accommodation, covert profiling to outright criminalization.

This contradiction of self in the society and self-negotiation in the world is a daily activity. The racially marginalized is constantly negotiating their friends, both racially and intra-racially. Racially marginalized persons have different perceptions and experiences. They constantly negotiate their lives, their existence, their geographical locations to soften the pain of social distortion and alienation against them. Their felt experience is existential because it concerns their sense of personhood.[221] The racialized is in the

---

[220] King, 1968, p. 102.

[221] Paul Tillich, *Systematic Theology. Vol. One* (London, The University of Chicago Press, 1951) 175: "The individual is a person in the sight of the law. The original meaning of the word persona, (*prosopon*) points to the actor's mask which makes him a definite character. Historically . . . Personal standing has been denied to slaves, children, and women. They have not attained full individualization in many cultures because they have been unable to participate fully; and, conversely, they have not been fully individualized. No process of emancipation was begun until the stoic philosophers fought successfully for the doctrine that every human being participates in the universal logos. The uniqueness of every person

"world" but in some way "above the world" experientially. They are above the world, and they are in the world at the same time. The racialized is nonetheless bound to the world and must negotiate their existence in the world.

It is not exactly what Jesus meant when he said in John 15:19: "If ye were of the world, the world would love its own; but because ye are not of the world, I have chosen you out of the world, therefore the world hateth you." The marginalized person is constantly negotiating an existential understanding of the world based on their sociopolitical and economic experience. How they are perceived, accepted, and accommodated in the concrete world. The racialized feels a sense of being thrown out of the world because of the social pricks of racism. They constantly negotiate their existence within a racialized social consciousness. The racially marginalized has a very intuitive consciousness regarding their environment and its perception of them. It is an existential consciousness socially engendered due to the felt experience of racial stigmatization. This consciousness is introspective as individuals find themselves in immediate contact with the source of their being. Instead of constantly turning outward and outside for hope and strength, they must turn inward and inside. They look within to negotiate their existence.

It is white America that has made being black so disconsolate an estate. Legal slavery may be in the past, but segregation and subordination have been allowed to persist. Even today, America imposes a stigma on every black child at birth.
(Andrew Hacker, 1992).

---

was not established until Christian churches acknowledged the universality of salvation and the potentiality of every human being to participate in it. This development illustrates the strict interdependence of individuality and participation on the level of complete individualization, which is, at the same time, the level of complete participation. The individual participated in his environment or, in the case of the complete individualization, in his world."

The Black person in the West "knows" himself or herself. He or she "knows" where to go and where not to go. It is not due to a sense of social dislocation, but a felt sense of rejection and suspicion that they are intuitively conscious of in the West. Thus, they must return to the person within that prefigures the person on the outside. This activity is constant, but the ones who perpetuate racism and its consciousness do not "know."

The question of self and identity is one that has been around for centuries. But this question for the Black person is important because it borders on skin color and race as the fundamental means of human identity in the West. The West's engagement in slavery and the slave trade has distorted its consciousness and imagination of human beings. To be human is to be validated through the prism of race and racism in the West. It is a distortion, specifically perpetuated and reflected in the United States' criminal justice system through mass incarceration.

St. Augustine's response to the question of identity is poignant. There is a claim for self-certainty that transcends race and material identity. A distorted self is healed when one takes possession of a consciousness of self that transcends the material understanding of self. It reflects a movement from the material self to the immaterial self. One's sense of self-certainty is firmly established when the immaterial self informs the material self. The Black child growing up in a society that has criminalized him before he comes to the consciousness of who he is must be told about who he really is, the one he does not see but is known by him.

It is in this context that St. Augustine's search for the authentic person is relevant: one that condemns a racialized understanding of humanity. For St. Augustine, certainty about self and the confidence associated with self-certainty is grounded in God. It is therapeutic and transformative. Presented in St. Augustine's analysis of self-certainty is a fundamental argument against the racialization of human beings. His analysis of self-certainty is an outright rejection of Hegel's argument of once a criminal always a criminal. Hegel's notion of crime and punishment rejects the possibility of a second chance for the offender. This view of crime and punishment reflects the agony of the Black man. St. Augustine differs from Hegel in that Augustine upholds the inherent worth of the person as fundamental to understanding every human being. He does not see the offender as an inherent criminal. The inherent worth of the person is rehabilitative because it is divine. For Augustine, this understanding of the other is grounded in a mystical relationship with the Divine.

Main Points:

- Mass incarceration leads to ontological distortion;
- Racialized mass incarceration in the United States devalues human beings.
- Mass incarceration in the U.S. perpetuates racial depersonalization.
- Mass incarceration in the U.S has historically reduced Blacks to a domesticated category.
- Mass incarceration in the U.S. reduces human beings to an instrumental value: simply to be used, abused and discarded.

St. Augustine: Self-Certainty and the Second Chance:

I am made 'black' only in the most superficial way by virtue of being the object of a white racist's hate. The emphatic exchange of survivors' tales among 'brothers,' even the collective struggle against the clear wrong of racism, does not provide a tapestry sufficiently rich to give meaning and definition to the totality of my life.
(Dr. Glenn C. Loury, 1993).

"What is self-certainty"? Augustine asked. How can I be certain that I am without appealing to material things or social status as the only source of my identity? Is self-certainty possible, and how can it be

117

attained? These were some of the "vexing" questions with which one of the greatest bishops Africa has produced struggled. It should be established that St. Augustine was not a European but a true African of the Berber tribe of North Africa. St. Augustine an African and, Bishop of Hippo in North Africa (AD 354-430), embarked upon answering this question during his long career as philosopher, theologian, writer, and leader of the Church in Africa. In the writings of this great African Bishop, we see a notion of self-certainty through the soul and its activities that not only seeks to ground rational human understanding of self in God, but also an ontological understanding that in Augustine's view, precedes one's racial justification of self and the other. Augustine's goal was to produce an understanding of self by referencing an interior understanding of self-based on one's relationship with God.[222] For Augustine, there is a certainty of self that is first grounded not only in the five senses but also in the intelligible knowledge of God.

Self-certainty for Augustine is consciousness, and this consciousness is of God within the consciousness of self. The soul that is ruled by God can rule the body. But never should the soul succumb ultimately to the body, its appetites, and desires, for the soul will then find itself under the control of the body. God as superior should rule the soul and not the "inferior," which is the body.[223] The more the soul finds intimacy with God, the more it comprehends the body and true self-certainty. For Augustine, submission to God is the path to deliverance, the path to "truth and happiness," to "achieve perfect mental health." To know God is to know self. This certainty and "beauty," he argues are given only to

---

[222] Edger Brightman, *Moral Law*, Plato was the first to assert an interior relationship in knowledge between the spiritual and physical world, 125.

[223] *On Music*, VI, 5, 12-13; (Trans. Tafford P. Maher, S.J., *The De Musica VI of St. Augustine*, Translated and Philosophically Annotated (St. Louis University Master's Thesis, 1939), 87-89.

those who enjoy the contemplation of God's eternal nature, to be moved and adorned by it, and to be able to merit eternal life."[224]

In Augustine's analysis, knowledge about the soul leads to the knowledge of God. The soul is spiritual, and the body is physical. Augustine establishes a distinction between the soul and the material world. He makes no "affirmation about the soul now except that it has come from God in such a way that it is not the substance of God and that it is incorporeal, that is, it is not a body but a spirit."[225] The soul is immaterial, incorporeal, and spiritual. Even at death, the soul does not die.

In explaining the role of the soul about self, Augustine argues that the soul has victory over the material world. The soul implies the totality of the human being, yet the soul and the body are one. He writes, "Whoever wishes to separate the body from human nature is a fool."[226] While the soul is naturally attracted to the body according to Augustine, "the soul seems to me to be a substance having rationality, which is fitted to the body to rule it." [227] Therefore, "man . . . is a rational soul using a mortal and earthly body."[228] In On the Trinity (400-416), he speaks definitively, "Man is a rational substance made up of soul and body . . . Man is, as the ancients said, a rational, mortal animal."[229] In essence, Augustine in this analysis is establishing the grounds for a coherent understanding of the person as a unit, holistic as body and soul, and intricately united.[230] The union of the soul and body for Augustine is a very

---

[224] *The True Religion*, 3.3; (Trans. C.A. Hangartner, S.J., De vera religione (Chapters 1-17) (St. Louis University Master's Thesis, 1945), pp. 9, 11. 126. Eugene Portalie, *A Guide To The Thought of Saint Augustine* (Chicago, Henry Regnery Company 1960). 146.

[225] Ibid., 147.

[226] Ibid., 147.

[227] Ibid. 147.

[228] Ibid., 147.

[229] Ibid., 147.

[230] Kelly Brown Douglas, *What's Faith Got to Do with It*, (New York, Orbis Books, 2005) 19-18. In reflecting on the root of the social stereotypes defining people of African descent in America, Kelly Brown Douglas in her book: *What's Faith Got to Do With It* poignantly analyzes the root of racism as the fundamental cause for how Black people are perceived. According to Douglas, the enslavement and lynching of black people among prominent

intricate union that provides life and being to the body. He writes, "The body, therefore, subsists through the soul and exists by the very fact that it is animated . . . The soul gives form to the body so that the latter is body insofar as it exists."[231] He writes "the body and soul are one man although the body and the soul are not one . . ."[232] To love God is to live above the passions of the body, but not to abandon the body since we exist in the concrete world. For Augustine, the soul must maintain its spirituality. The union between the soul and the body is spiritual and mystical, which no human being can understand. The soul is indistinguishable from the body because they are one.[233] He argues that a better understanding of the soul leads to a better understanding of self.

Augustine establishes the spiritual understanding of self-certainty as a basis for the interior life and the physical life. For Augustine, this is the ground of selfhood, of personhood, and true self-identity. This is the true ground for human identity. It transcends the material body, for the material body cannot be all

---

causes in America could be attributed to the division between the body and the soul predominant in Western philosophy and influenced by Rene Descartes. She argues that the American church was able to condone slavery and participate in the lynching of black bodies because Douglas argues, whites at the time believed that black bodies dualistically were highly inferior to white bodies. Secondly, since salvation was mainly concerned with the soul and not the body, blacks were prevented from baptism by white churches in the days of slavery and lynching. The understanding was that if blacks were baptized, they would be considered Christians and their souls saved. To save the black soul meant accommodating and accepting the black person as a person like any other white person and not enslaving, racializing or lynching them. Therefore, Douglas argues, to justify the lynching of black people, to keep them enslaved and radicalized, the Church prevented black people from baptism, from the Eucharist and the preaching of the gospel. In that case, their bodies could be lynched and their souls unsaved. These were some of the reasons for the rebellion of black ministers to organize the Black Church. "In theological understanding, dualism connotes a particular kind of relationship. It commonly refers to an oppositional/antagonistic way of relating. In a dualistic relationship mutuality of difference is precluded. Dualistic paradigm places contrasting objects or elements into hostile and /or hierarchical overpowered, dominated, or not respected by the other. One element is typically revered while the other is vilified; one is considered good and the other evil."

[231] Portalie., 147.
[232] Ibid., 147.
[233] Ibid., 148

there is about the human being. To derive selfhood simply based on the material is to deny identity to self. It is a recipe for subjugation and ill-treatment. The person is more than what the eye beholds. In his quest, Augustine inquires,

> How then am I to seek for you, Lord? When I seek for you, my God, my quest is for the happy life. I will seek you that 'my soul may live,' for my body derives life from my soul, and my soul derives life from you. How then shall I seek for the happy life? It is not mine until I say: 'It is enough, it is there."[234]

For Augustine, this search underscores his argument that the human being is made in the image of God with a spiritual self-called the soul that establishes the identity of every human being. Augustine must look within himself to find himself. As he turned away from what he was doing that turned him away from God, in himself, he found God, and in himself, he found himself. He writes,

> With you as my guide, I entered into my innermost citadel (himself) and was given power to do so because you had become my helper. I entered and with my soul's eye, such as it was, saw above that same eye of my soul the immutable light higher than my mind—not the light of every day, obvious to anyone . . . It was not that light, but a different thing, utterly different from all our kind of light . . . It was superior because it made me, and I was inferior because I was made by it. The person who knows the truth knows it, and he who knows it knows eternity . . . When I first came to know you, you raised me up to make me see that what I saw is Being and that I who saw am not yet Being. And you gave a shock to the weakness of my sight; by the strong radiance of your rays I trembled with love and awe. And I found myself far from you "in the region of dissimilarity," and heard as it were your voice from on high: "I am the food of the fully grown; grow and you will feed on me. And you will not change

---

[234] St. Augustine, *Confessions* (Trans. Henry Chadwick, Oxford, Oxford University Press, 1991) Book V11: X (16).

me into you like the food your flesh eats, but you will be changed into me."[235]

Augustine has stumbled upon something that he cannot "comprehend." The source of who he really "is" is immaterial. But Augustine is aware that in the process of deriving true self-identity, he must return to the material, to the body because the body is not an enemy of self; both exist holistically. According to Augustine, possessing this understanding of self is self-liberating. It is liberating for the individual who comes to the consciousness of this knowledge and perceives others as such. Not only do we see in Augustine an adequate definition of selfhood, but we also see that the lack of this understanding of self can only lead to the internalization of what society says about you and what society perpetuates about you. It is in this context that we see a lot of Black youths internalizing several of the negative images about the self that distorts their true sense of being. The consequence, if one is not careful, is to manifest the internalized images in ways that are incompatible with one's true self. Stereotypes are socially constructed, socially promoted, and fundamentally influential in the formulation of policies, the construction of meaning, and identity. The images they promote ultimately result in the objectification of the other person and their reduction to thinghood. It is in this context that we can understand the high rates of arrest, detention, and incarceration of Black men and their social implications.

Self-certainty is within; its "grounds" is divine. The human being is profound. The inherent dignity of the human being is not based on Black or White, Brown or Yellow, Pink or Blue, money or no money, food or no food, education or no education, job or no job, criminal or noncriminal record, offender or non-offender record, and victim or no victim. The person simply "is." Augustine's theological analysis of self-certainty rejects the consciousness that racializes the other, thus reducing one to "thinghood." For Augustine, the person simply "is"—an ontological being of inherent worth and dignity. For

---

[235] Ibid., *Book X: xix* (29).

Hegel, the criminal will always be a criminal because crime once committed defines the criminal's identity and essentially stigmatizes him/her in the concrete world of socio-political activities. For St. Augustine: "All have sinned and fallen short of the glory of God, and are justified freely by God's grace through the redemption that came by Christ Jesus." (Romans 3:23-25).

> ***Do I need to appear 'Black,' in the manner in which blacks are negatively portrayed in the media, to be considered 'Black'?... I am an educated, well-spoken black woman. My race is one of my many attributes: neither limiting, nor defining. I represent the culmination of my experiences, and the many cultures that have influenced me. I represent the colors of my ancestors. But most of all, I represent myself, and of that, I am most proud.***
> (Renee Delphin, 1997).

Main points:
- To know self is to be certain of self.
- Self-certainty is superior to racial certainty.
- Self-certainty is self-liberating.
- For Hegel, the criminal is forever criminalized.
- For Augustine: We are all criminals: the criminal is a candidate for a second chance. We are all crimina

The Groundless Me`
    I must return to myself and find me`
    The me of myself in me
    Since the me you see needs me`
    I shall relinquish myself to furnish me`
    The me` of groundless me`
    Since the me you need is me`
    -the groundless me`
    I will respond to the me` in me
    The myself of me`
    Since the me` of me is myself
    Reduce me not to the me you see

For the me you see needs me`
The me` unseen-the groundless me`.
(George Walters-Sleyon)

Similarly, Pope John Paul II advances the argument for a holistic understanding of every human being. The Pope presents a critique of the socially constructed notion of human beings and its distortion of what he calls the "culture of being."

Pope John Paul II

Racism is… a negation of the deepest identity of the human being, who is a person created in the image and likeness of God.
(Pope John Paul, 1997).

Suspicious of the twentieth century's materialistic understanding of the person, John Paul II contends that the dignity of the person firmly rests on the concept of the image of God [236] present in every human being. The image of God is the only possible means of understanding individuals as human beings and not as mere creatures. For the Pope, and St. Augustine, Christ's incarnation and crucifixion reflect the importance of humanity in God's divine plan. He writes,

> In reality, it is only in the mystery of the Word made flesh that the mystery of man truly becomes clear . . . Christ the new Adam, in the very revelation of the mystery of the Father and of his love, fully reveals man to himself and brings to light his most high calling . . . Human nature, by the very fact that it was assumed, not absorbed, in him, has been raised in us also to a

---

[236] Fr. Thomas McGovern, *The Christian Anthropology of John Paul 11: An Overview* www.Christendomawake.org/pages/mcgovern/chrisanthro.htm35.

dignity beyond compare. For, by his incarnation, he, the Son of God, has in a certain way united himself with each man.[237]

The Pope can only talk about "human flourishing" and what it means from the perspective of the incarnation of Jesus Christ. He speaks as someone who experienced the carnage of war, its psychological impact, and has seen the impact of human cruelty towards other. The incarnation is important because it uncovers the divine nature and destiny of the human being.[238] Humanity is revealed in Christ. The Pope argues that human beings are created in the image of God. It provides the basis for a concept of solidarity and mutual understanding. It is within this context that we can develop a healthy mindset about every human being. The Pope condemns assumptions and perceptions that breed inequalities, subjugation, war, hunger, illiteracy, and oppression. His condemnation of the social crisis of the world reflects his rejection of the prevailing trend of economic disparities reflective of the world today with the concentration of wealth in the hands of few individuals while the majority lingers in poverty. It reflects the link between the social conditions of poverty, marginalization, racism, illiteracy, alienation, injustice, crime, violence, social unrest, distrust, apathy and mass incarceration. Pope John Paul II condemns the consumer-based notion of life that has emerged as contributing to the commodification and distortion of what he calls the "culture of being." Speaking in 1987 in Chile, Pope John Paul II asserted his call for the recognition of the true value of every human being. He writes,

> A process of reflection is necessary, which leads to a renewed diffusion and defense of the fundamental values of man as man,

---

[237] Vatican Council 11, Gaudium et Spes (GS) (The Church in the Modern World, 1965) and Dignitatis Humanae (Decree on Religious Freedom, 1965). 22.

[238] An over view www. Christendom-awake.org/pages/mcgovern/chrisanthro.htm.) Fr. McGovern,

and in relation to other persons and to the natural surroundings in which he lives.[239]

Finally, for Pope John Paul II, the person is a human being who is in "solidarity" with other persons with the goal of arriving at the "common good." In St. Augustine's argument for self-certainty, we see the rejection of the devaluation of the person to thinghood, propagated by the prison-industrial complex.

In summary, St. Augustine and Pope John Paul II assert the claim of one's relationship to God as the source of human origin. It is the struggle for human dignity and the quest to establish the ontological ground for human dignity. The process is reflected in the passion to assert a recognition for human dignity in the face of debilitating circumstances engendered, for example, by mass incarceration. St. Augustine's process of deriving knowledge about the self leads to an introspective understanding of self-certainty. He begins by looking within, for within, one finds the grounds for self-certainty. This exercise for St. Augustine is primary to the process of self understanding. Mass incarceration is not adequately understood without an understanding of the process of stigmatization and how human beings are perceived in the United States. As Muelder intimates, penal sentencing in the United States is associated with the interests of vengeful penology and financial gain.[240]

It is in this context that one can adequately understand the conviction and sentiments expressed in John Wesley's letter to William Wilberforce in Wilberforce's fight for the abolition of slavery and the slave trade. He writes,

Dear Sir:

Unless the divine power has raised you, for us to be *a Athanasius contra mundum*, I see not how you can go through your glories

---

[239] John Paul 11, *"The Task of the World Culture of Today Is to Promote the Civilization of Love"* (3 April 1987) no. 4, in English language weekly edition of L'Osservatore Romano (4 May 1987): 5.

[240] (Wogaman, 2007)

enterprise in opposing that execrable villainy which is the scandal of religion, of England, and of human nature. Unless God has raised you up for this very thing, you will be worn out by the opposition of men and devils. But if God be for you, who can be against you? Are all of them together stronger than God? O be not weary of well-doing! Go on, in the name of God and in the power of his might, till even American slavery (the vilest that ever saw the sun) shall vanish away before it. Reading this morning a tract written by a poor African, I was particularly struck by that circumstance that a man who has a black skin, being wronged or outraged by a white man, can have no redress; it being a 'law' in our colonies that the oath of a black against a white goes for nothing. What villainy is this? [241]

Wesley wrote to encourage Wilberforce in the fight to end slavery because Wesley understood the nature and principles of true justice, fairness, and equality. He knew that the one who holds the Scripture in high esteem should also know that every mortal being has the spark of God within them. For Wesley, adding his voice and prayers to the fight for the recognition of the divine foundation of every human being was that ultimate push for justice. He understood the shared mutuality of human connectedness. Wesley's advocacy against slavery was based on the conviction that the essence of the slaves as human beings was not material and profit based but immaterial.

I dwell in the Permanent
For the Pre-eminent is within
To dwell in the permissive is to dwindle in perplexity
Therefore I gasp at profundity and wither the paralysis
(George Walters-Sleyon)

---

[241] http://gbgm-umc.org/umw/Wesley/wilber.stm, Wesley's Thoughts on Slavery: http://docsouth.unc.edu/church/wesley/wesley.html, http://www.historyy.ucsb.edu/faculty/marcuse/classes/2c/texts/17, http://gbgm-umc.org/umw/wesley/thoughtsuponslavery.stm

In the search for the authentic person, in Augustine, we find a cogent theological analysis of self and the quest for self-certainty that is fundamental to the Black person's sense of personhood. But in Dr. W. E. B. Du Bois, we find the quest for answers to another question, a question regarding the racialized person.

W. E. B. Du Bois and the Racialized Person

Being a Negro in American means being herded in ghettos, or reservations, being constantly ignored and made to feel invisible. You long to be seen, to be heard, to be respected. But it is like blowing in the wind. As I think about the anatomy of the ghetto, I am often reminded of a passage from W. E. B. Du Bois' autobiography, Dusk of Dawn:

'It is difficult to let others see the full psychological meaning of caste segregation. It is as though one, looking out from a dark cave in a side of an impending mountain, sees the world passing and speaks to it; speaks courteously and persuasively, showing them how these entombed souls are hindered in their natural movement, expression, and development and how their loosening from prison would be a matter not simply of courtesy, sympathy, and help to them, but aid to all the world.'
(Martin Luther King, Jr. *Where Do We Go From Here: Chaos or Community, p.110).*

Why is the person of African descent in America or the Diaspora interested in the questions of race? In *The Conservation of Races*, Du Bois asserts that the Black person in America has always felt the need to discuss the "destinies and origins of the races primarily because in the back of most discussions of race with which he is familiar, have lurked certain assumptions as to his natural abilities, as to his political, intellectual and moral status which he felt were wrong." [242] Du Bois defines race as a "social construction" influenced by environmental and social factors. He was forever critical of the use of race for the justification of evil perpetrated against Blacks in the name of self-defense. Du Bois gave four reasons why race antagonism was used as a justification:

- **First**: A "repulsion" from something "evil" or "harmful" and therefore it is an instrument of survival.
- **Second**: "A reasonable measure of self-defense against undesirable racial traits."
- **Third**: Racial antipathy is a method of race development."
- **Finally**: Race antipathy is a conscious "method of group specialization" (Du Bois: *Does Race Antagonism Serve Any Good Purpose*, published in 1914 in *The Crisis*).

Under these conditions, the Black person in America is caught in a psychological malady in search of their identity.

Du Bois coined the phrase *"Double consciousness"* to capture the "pain" of existential "Blackness." It reflects an existential experience that tries to capture the sense of nothingness. Double consciousness implies an inner tension within one's self. The Black person's selfhood is defined about external factors that contradict their true sense of being. Double consciousness is a scrutinizing experience of self that questions one's sense of self-worth and humanity. It is the perception that the Black person is an illusion, to be seen, but not to be heard. Double consciousness is living behind the veil. According to Du Bois,

> The Negro is a sort of seventh son, born with a veil, and gifted with second-sight in this American world, -a world which yields him no true self-consciousness, but only lets him see himself

---

[242] Phil Zuckerman. *The Social Theory of W.E.B. Du Bois*, (London: Pine Forge Press, 2004) 19. Du Bois, W. E. B. *The Conservation of Races:* Published in 1897 in the *Occasional Papers of the America Negro Academy.*

through the revelation of the other world, it is a peculiar sensation, this double-consciousness, this sense of always

Looking at one's self through the eyes of others, of measuring one's soul by the type of world that looks on in amused contempt and pity. One feels his two-ness—an American, a Negro; two souls, two thoughts, two unreconciled strivings; two warring ideals in one dark body, whose dogged strength alone keeps it from being torn asunder (Du Bois: *The Souls of Black Folk*, pg. 2).

Double consciousness is the dilemma facing the Black person, to be "White." It is the contradiction of being a part, yet an "other," of being an insider, but an outsider, or of knowing oneself to be a subject, yet regarded as an object. It is conforming to White culture but confined to Black culture, the tension to be judged by White paradigms while delighting in Black pride, the frustration of being oneself, but considered a duplicate, and the anguish of overt acceptance yet sensing covert rejection and restrictions. Double consciousness is the experience of nothingness, the limitation of self, an existential despair of coming to the end of one's options and alternatives, but only with the fear of doom and nothingness. Double consciousness captures the subtle agony of the Black person as fractured by several social roles and identities that are often in tension with one another while struggling to remain certain of self.

Those who have crossed this threshold through academic, social, and material advancement know what it means, yet are haunted by the scars of two-ness. But Du Bois must articulate this hopelessness of self in the presence of pain, as well as the threat of self by self. Self is presented as an opposition to itself instead of self-affirming itself, the threat of being by nonbeing in its brutal torture of me in me, the I in me to the point of subtle agony. To experience double consciousness is to experience the pain of racism, racialization, racial profiling, thinghood, objectification, and mass incarceration. It is to be interpreted simply based on one's Blackness. To understand the magnitude of this experience is to delve into the subtle scrutiny and suspicion that confronts the dreams and aspirations of Black men, especially, in the United States. It is the suspicion associated with every transaction of the Black entrepreneur, and that suspicion reduces to psychological Blackness every achievement of the Black intellectual. Du Bois, like the melancholic poet, must lament the meaninglessness of this experience. It is because the Black person is asked to empty himself of his African heritage. He is asked to pour out of himself his Blackness. He is asked to purify himself of his Negro-ness. He is asked to purify himself of himself, and since such a request entails the distortion of his sense of consciousness, Du Bois must bring into absurdity the meaninglessness of such a request and exclaim:

> What, after all, am I? Am I an American or am I a Negro? Can I be both? Or is it my duty to cease to be a Negro as soon as possible and be an American? If I strive as a Negro, am I not perpetuating the very cleft that threatens and separates Black and White America? Is not my only possible practical aim the seduction of all that is Negro in me to the American? Does my black blood place upon me any more obligations to assert my nationality than German, or Irish or Italian blood would? (Du Bois, *The Conservation of Race*).

For Du Bois, this is the source of his inner-dividedness. He is forced to look continuously within himself. Du Bois, like Augustine, must travel on an introspective path, one that involves the looking within. Both were great intellectuals of astute minds and intelligence, yet both must be introspective to find the "Ground of their being," the root of their humanity, and the river of their being to assert self as self. For Augustine, it was a religious journey of conversion. Augustine was interested in knowing God because of which he could know himself. Du Bois was on a journey to understand self, considering his sociopolitical and economic debilitations. His journey was philosophical, existential, and spiritual.

Du Bois must question his sense of being in an environment that saw the color of his skin solely for who he was within his Black race, as his limitation. Only if he were White, would he be accepted?

He must question his existence and ask for responses, and because responses could not readily be found, he resorts to the liberty of the pen, the typewriter, and the writing pad. Du Bois' search for answers and the authentic self was not simply a philosophical inquiry to satisfy his rational ego. Du Bois' existential inquiry was to discover self and answers, which his existential location demanded. This existential search for self permeated his being, creating in him the angst of unjust treatment faced by the Black person on the street, in the ghettos, in the alleys, the cells, the prisons, the detention facilities, and the fields. Like them, he must become restless until he tells their story, articulates their anxieties, and captures their despair in words, with his soul, his heart, and his pen.

Du Bois came to understand the Black experience as a collective experience. In attempting to articulate this inner demise, this splitting of oneself within, he saw racism as a problem that was becoming both global and devastating. He argued that it was a problem that blinded the eyes of its perpetrators, deafened the ears of those who championed it, and hardened the hearts of those it benefitted. The benefit, privilege, status, and power racism accrue must flow ceaselessly for generations to come while it afflicts the lives of its victims. He saw the life of the racist and the racialized as two painful lives, characterized by the departure from integration to disintegration, from similarity to dissimilarity, and from unity to disunity. Racism, tribalism, and other forms of exclusionary consciousness resist the need to recognize the idea of shared human connectedness and mutuality. The cord that holds humanity in oneness must be fractured, broken, and eventually abandoned. Du Bois articulates this pain in the face of the racialization of self in opposition to self to avoid self-distortion. He cannot stand this duplicity and the cognitive dissonance of self toward self, occurring within himself. He knows that tension often arises between those who recognize this shared mutuality by existing interdependently and those who refuse to recognize it and desire to perpetuate a distorted view of humanity for self-interest. Du Bois saw racism as a major problem in the West with its tentacles spreading to other continents. He writes,

The problem of the twentieth century is the problem of the color-line-the relation of the darker to the lighter races of men in Asia and Africa, in America and the islands of the sea." (Du Bois, *The Souls of Black Folk* pg. 9).

Du Bois' painstaking social analysis investigated issues of power imbalance in the 19th and 20th centuries. For Du Bois, the "color line belts the world."[243] In his analysis, separation based on race is the determining factor in the formulation of sociopolitical, economic, and religious policies and practices. The color line determines Black/White social relationships.

One cannot dismiss the fact that Du Bois was a pioneer. The gloomy picture of the late nineteenth and early twentieth centuries reflecting the demise of Black people has been greatly altered. Blacks have been able to penetrate certain socio-political and economic structures that were mere dreams to Du Bois and others, though they were very optimistic about the intellectual potential of Blacks. The United States has had a Black president in the person of Barack H. Obama, a great accomplishment considering the history of this country. Nonetheless, how do we explain the mass incarceration of Blacks and Hispanics, especially of Black men, youth and the growing incarceration of Black women in the United States in the 21st century compared to the angsts of slavery?

The above analysis is an attempt to articulate the historical consciousness of racism and criminalization in the United States as evident in the mass incarceration of Blacks in the 21st century. It is an attempt to derive a way of speaking to a bewildered group of men and women with their sense of identity, destiny, and understanding undermined by racial sentencing, criminalization, racial profiling, and punishment as a means of profit making not restoration.

The Black Church has historically served as a "city of refuge" for the community. The birth of the Black Church is characterized by the Black experience of slavery and anxiety in America. It must be willing to intervene once again by advocating for true justice,

---

[243] Eric Sundquist, *W. E. B Du Bois Reader*. (Oxford: Oxford University Press, 1994) 6.

fairness and equality. With the exception that this time, it is not only for Black men and women as African Americans but also for Blacks as African immigrants from Africa and the Caribbean lingering between indefinite detention and indefinite deportation.

> ***The ability to remain true to one self… must begin with the ethical project of considering how we can align a sense of ourselves with a sense of the world. This is the essence of integrity, is it not, never having to split into a well-maintained 'front' and a closely guarded 'inside' … In its most literal sense, the ability to be one person rather than two refers to some resolution of the ethically dangerous position of finding oneself split between the one one is and the one one feels one has to be. The sheltered self and the masquerade.***
> (Patricia Williams, 1997, from Ella Mazel: *"And don't call me a racist!"*).

Main Points

- Racialized mass incarceration distorts the Spark of the Divine within.
- The fight against mass incarceration in the U.S. must employ the principles consistent with the struggles to end slavery and Jim Crow.

- Mass Black incarceration in the United States reflects the angst of America's racial consciousness and its historic exploitation of Black humanity.
- The "problem of the color line" continues to influence and define the American criminal justice system.
- "Double Consciousness" is an articulation of the existential angst of being Black in the American social consciousness and its socio-cultural and economic debilitations.

It is not a case of our people...wanting either separation or integration. The use of these words actually clouds the real picture. The 22 million Afro-Americans don't seek either separation or integration. They seek recognition and respect as human beings.
(Malcolm X).

A PRESCRIPTIVE DISCUSSION

CHAPTER SEVEN
A Call to the Black Church

The movement of the Spirit of God in the hearts of men often calls them to act against the spirit of their times or causes them to anticipate a spirit which is yet in the making. In a moment of dedication, they are given wisdom and courage to dare a deed that challenges and to kindle a hope that inspires.
(Howard Thurman: *Footprints of a Dream*).

The Black Church has historically been the harbinger of the Black religious experience. Its pivotal role as a place of refuge for the weary soul cannot be overstated. The Black Church has withstood social forces to construct its identity and reality. Whether socially imposed from above or social forces generated from within, the Black Church has been able to interpret its existence within the context of these forces meaningfully. The Black Church has also engendered the construction of social forces that have shaped the social ethos of America. In its intrinsic experience of God and the translation of the knowledge of that experience within the context of its social location, the Black Church has withstood its encroachment from outside. Through the shared experience of the transcendent presence of God in their midst, a synthesis of beliefs and practices used to construct meaning for individuals and collective initiatives has evolved to serve as a refuge for its troubled souls. For the Black Church, religious experience is ineffable, mental, social, transcendental, and phenomenological. The spiritual context is the engagement with God. The communal context is the Black Church and the context for the construction of meaning and interpretation of its social reality. It consists of the existential experiences and implications of slavery, segregation, racism, Black-on-Black crime, HIV/AIDS, mass incarceration, concentrated poverty, triumphs, victory, failures, and successes. According to Dale Andrews, the "refuge" image of the Black Church is the historical interpretation of the existential role of the Black Church in the Black community. While resisting what he refers to as "adversarial posturing and deafness"[244] on the part of those who criticize the Black Church as being only "other-worldly," Andrews contends that

> This image includes concerns for the survival, nurture, and growth of African Americans through the Christian faith. The church fulfilled the emotional, spiritual, and sociological needs of an alienated people. It provided a community that affirmed and nurtured black community, black humanity and worth in an otherwise hostile and degrading social existence. This safe space was not static. Community provided proactive space for personality development and human relations. The effect was empowerment for living anew.[245]

He argues that the refuge image emerged as a "corporate identity."[246] fostered in the midst of slavery and discrimination for the benefit of "both human and spiritual bonding" and "human community and relatedness."[247] Andrews argues that the Black Church "has commonly fostered Black wholeness and human

---

[244] Dale Andrews, *Practical Theology For Black Churches: Bridging Black Theology and African American Folk Religion* (Louisville: Westminster John Knox Press, 2002) 9.

[245] Ibid., 34.

[246] Ibid., 35.

[247] Ibid., 35.

rights."[248] Against the criticism of being simply concerned with nonsocial activities, the Black Church has asserted itself as a "protective community" in the midst of discrimination and racism. It has done so by establishing a "sociopolitical presence" developed as a place "for the critical affirmation of human value and human needs, which included liberation."[249] The Black Church, therefore, finds itself responsible for preaching spiritual salvation and social salvation- "spiritual faith and liberation."[250] It is the cultivation of both "spiritual and social liberation"[251] for the holistic liberation of the Black person. Andrews argues that "liberation can begin only in the Black community"[252] through the Black Church translating the liberating message of the gospel of Jesus Christ into concrete actions.

Commenting on the origin of the Black Church, Emmanuel McCall argues that the despair and anguish of racism are the "birth pang of the Black church."[253] It became a Black Church because of the experience of slavery, in which slaves and ex-slaves were attempting to make sense of their sociopolitical, social-cultural, and economic conditions. But not only were these experiences pivotal to the formation of what is now referred to as the Black Church, but the fact also remains that slaves and ex-slaves could not be allowed to "worship God" together with their White masters. While various slaves' and ex-slaves' worship communities eventually assumed the identities of their former masters' denominations, they transformed the borrowed practices to reflect their existential experiences. It is in this light that what is called the Black Church emerged. In describing the theological thrust of the Black Church, McCall argues that "the practicing of religion for the Black church is a theology of survival . . . I must underscore the fact that the Black Church is the

---

[248] Ibid., 35.
[249] Ibid., 36.
[250] Ibid., 36.
[251] Ibid., 8.
[252] Ibid., 36.
[253] Charles Foster, *Black Religious Experience: Conversation on Double Consciousness and The work of Grant Shockley* (Nashville, Abingdon, 2003). 9.

carrier of black folk culture. If you want true authentic American Black culture, you must go to the Black church."[254] The Black Church was a source of social unity, serving as a sociocultural and educational center. The Black Church then, and in several ways today, provides communal wholeness. It serves as the center for social and spiritual activities. He writes, "When the world and the society in which we lived were constantly tearing us apart, the church continued to help us to get it together, to 'get it all together.'"[255]

The "two-ness" of the social reality of Black people have also shaped the Black religious experience. It is existence on two levels of consciousness, historically influenced and religiously influenced. Understanding this "dual existence" is fundamental to understanding the root of the Black religious experience. This understanding existentially provides the religious and social contexts for the construction of meaning. But this socio-religious construction of reality does not simply take place in the "public sphere" but the Black Church. It provides the context for individual and collective character and theological formation. Commenting on the pivotal role of the Black Church, Grant Shockley writes:

> In their sermons, spirituals, prayers and Sunday school teachings, Black people came to terms with their blackness, their expressional gifts, and their social situation of slavery and brutalizing oppression in a white-racist church and society. There is where they "worked out their salvation" in relation to questions of their bondage, their separation from family, their chattel status, their idea of good and evil, of God and Satan. From its beginning in the time of slavery, the church came to have a particular significance to black people because it provided them with a "gathered community" of relative freedom, expressional outlet, community information, group

---

[254] Foster, *Black Religious Experience*. 13.
[255] Ibid., 14.

Solidarity, personal affirmation, mutual aid, and leadership development.[256]

The Black Church became a meeting place, an opportunity for the creation of social ideas and meaning, the construction of identity and selfhood, and the impetus for social relevance and action. The Black Church became a "second community" for African Americans living in the twilight of despair, characterized by the search for "somebodiness." This "two-ness" is understood as life in the non-church community and the church community, as a negation of selfhood and acceptance, in the Black Church where one is affirmed and in the non-church community where one is, and is "not." This two-ness characterizes the Black religious experience. It is this process of becoming, of pursuing selfhood and personhood, both on the individual and collective levels- in the sociopolitical and economic worlds that meaning is constructed by the Black man or woman. The Black Church is that place where meaningful construction takes place. Individuals could forge a sense of identity. It is done based on the secured space provided from the storms raging on the outside, the bewilderment, the estrangement and the conflict with self-experienced individually and collectively. Dr. Cornel West refers to this experience as "nihilism." Moving beyond the detached philosophical understanding of nihilism, West defines nihilism as "the lived experience of coping with a life of horrifying meaninglessness, hopelessness, and (most important) lovelessness."[257] As an age-old problem for Blacks in America, nihilism reflects the threat to being, selfhood, the me of me by the absurd. But West is very particular about the role of the Black Church as an enduring buffer against the raging storms from the outside. He writes,

> The genius of our black foremothers and forefathers was to create powerful buffers to ward off the nihilistic threat, to equip black folk with cultural armor to bear back the demons of

---

[256] Ibid., 32.
[257] Cornel West, *Race Matters* (New York: Vintage Books, 2001), 22-23.

hopelessness, meaninglessness, and lovelessness. These buffers consisted of cultural structures of meaning and feeling that created and sustained communities; this armor constituted ways of life and struggle that embodied values of service and sacrifice, love and care, discipline and excellence. In other words, traditions for blacks surviving and thriving under usually adverse New World conditions were major barriers against the nihilistic threat.[258]

However, West laments the fact that things are not the way they use to be. He blurts out the inevitable question, "What has changed? What went wrong?"[259]

These are some of the most pivotal questions that the Black Church through its preachers, pastors, deacons, deaconesses, and eventually, its members should ponder as we search for solutions to the predicament of mass Black incarceration. In his search for answers, West makes a cogent argument for "the saturation of market forces and market moralities in Black life and the present crisis in Black leadership."[260] One can argue that a level of insensitivity and apathy has emerged as a major obstacle in the Black community. The result is indifference and detachment to one another's plight. The number one social problem of the 21st century for the Black Church is the issue of Black mass incarceration. According to King, it is the responsibility of the Church to condemn the "immorality" of structural discrimination. In the process, it is called to: "affirm that every human life is a reflection of divinity, and that every act of injustice mars and defaces the image of God in man...The church must take the lead in social reform."[261] He intimates that the church's call to social transformation cannot be compromised or traded for the status quo.

---

[258] Ibid., 24.
[259] Ibid., *Race Matters*. 24.
[260] Ibid., 24.
[261] King, 1968, p. 99.

The gospel of Jesus Christ is represented most authentically in the liberation of the world's oppressed peoples from their bondage. The gospel is not an otherworldly escape from the hard realities of this world. Rather, it addresses those realities directly, empowering the oppressed to seize control of their own destiny and to establish a new order of freedom and justice.
(J. Philip Wogaman, *Christian Perspective on Politics*, p. 80).

Mass Black Incarceration is responsible for:

- A steady increase in HIV/AIDS epidemic in the Black Community.
- A breakdown of the Black family structure.
- A significant increase in single parenting and fatherlessness.
- A breakdown of the Black community.
- And increase in Black poverty and intergenerational impoverishment.

How can the Church respond to this catastrophe plaguing the Black community? Black men have been disproportionally incarcerated in times past in the United States. The difference in this era of incarceration is that many Black men are coming out of jails and prisons across the United States infected with HIV/AIDS, syphilis, etc. According to Human Rights Watch reports, there are good reasons to believe that there are substantial links between mass incarceration and the AIDS epidemic in the Black community. Consensual sex and non-consensual sex because of rape takes place in prison without condoms.

If human redemption is the thrust of the gospel provided by the life, death, and resurrection of Jesus Christ, the Church should then ask itself- what the meaning of this claim of the gospel for the situation today is? How can an adequate translation of the gospel of Jesus Christ speak to the existential, sociopolitical and economic conditions engendered by mass Black incarceration in the United States of America?

The mission of the Church is to reach out to the world with the gospel of Jesus Christ. This evangelistic responsibility does not negate the Church's social responsibility. In fact, the mission and evangelistic responsibility are in several ways compatible. This compatibility has always provided the foundation for which the Church exists.

Andrews argues that the "care for others" must be primary to the "care for selves."[262] He contends that the growth of membership in churches in our day and time does not tally with the awareness of social concerns reflected in the growing social demands. While most churches declare their intention for starting a "social ministry," their definition of social ministry often borders on internal concerns rather than external social concerns that affect the needs of the entire community. Andrews blames this kind of communal apathy on the permeation and centralization of American individualism in the Black Church's religious existence. As a practical theologian, Andrews sees the solution in what he calls "prophetic preaching." He writes,

> In this cultural milieu, black churches have lost the covenant relation between spiritual intimacy with God and human care for others. American individualism disrupts God's will for humanity as revealed in the prophetic inspiration of a covenant community. Personal salvation is not the goal of redemption history; it is a 'beginning again.' Prophetic preaching not only insists upon human care but also maintains the correlation between human reflexivity and theological relationality, which characterizes prophetic consciousness. Prophetic ministry unites worship and praxis, salvation and social justice.[263]

The present predicament of increasing incarceration and detention of Black men in America calls for the cultivation of ministries that are intentional in providing realistic solutions and answers. While the influence of the Black Church in the lives of the

---

[262] Andrews, 130

[263] Ibid., 130

present generation may not be as it was in the 1950s or the 1960s; Black churches should be intentional in reaching out to Black men and Black women with the goal to also save and heal the Black family. It means implementing programs that are biblically centered, yet socially relevant. It is in this context that I present the next chapter as a search for tangible, realistic and workable solutions to the "Situation."

Main Points:

- The Black Church is a place of refuge.
- The Black Church is a place of solidarity.
- The Black Church is a community.
- The Black Church must be proactive in dismantling mass incarceration.
- The Black Church should work to save the Black family from mass Black incarceration.
- The Black Church must engage in strategic solution development and implementations to reduce if not eliminate the long-term negative implications of mass Black incarceration on the Black community.

CHAPTER EIGHT
What Do We Do?

First, the line of progress is never straight. For a period a movement may follow a straight line and then it encounters obstacles and the path bends. It is like curving around a mountain when you are approaching a city. Often it feels as though you were moving backward, and you lose sight of your goal; but in fact you are moving ahead, and soon you will see the city again, closer by.
(Martin Luther King, Jr. *Where Do We Go From Here*, p.12).

This chapter advances four responses fundamental to the process of strategic solution development.

- The Prophetic response
- The Critical response
- The Rational response
- The Pragmatic response

These four responses are not exhaustive. They are reference points to begin the dialogue about dismantling mass incarceration in the United States of America.

A Prophetic Response

Theology is a progressive and continuous understanding, which is variable to a certain extent. If it were merely the understanding of abstract truth, this would not be true. If theology is the understanding of an existential stance, it is progressive, it is the understanding of a commitment in history concerning the Christian's location in the development of humanity and the living out of faith. Theology is a reflection that is, it is a second act, a turning back, a reflecting, that comes after action. Theology is not first; the commitment is first.
(Gustavo Gutierrez –*Toward A Theology of Liberation*).

Sentencing in the United States' criminal justice system is racially skewed. This skewness in the criminal justice system leads to higher rates of incarceration of those for whom justice also is skewed. In the process, justice is racially defined, racially executed and racially perpetuated. It leads to the distortion of human dignity and the violation of human rights.

A prophetic response argues for the respect for human dignity in the American criminal justice and prison systems. To reduce other human beings simply to race and execute justice on this basis is to embark upon a process of ontological distortion. This form of distortion fundamentally destroys their self-image. It perpetuates their criminalization and racialization in the eyes of others.[264]

Inherent dignity in every human being is also divine dignity. Justice subjected to racial particularities inversely undermines the

---

[264] Matt. 25: 40: The criminalization of the Black man is one of the greatest fears of the Black male professional. Regardless of his qualifications and personal development, his achievements are constantly subjected to criminalizing and suspicious scrutinies. He must strive to excel but is often caught in this dilemma of not doing his best because his best is often racially scrutinized.

147

concept of inherent dignity as well as divine dignity. It is this interpretation of justice that Jesus condemned as the worst expression of injustice in human social relationships.

Considering his imminent crucifixion and ultimate return, Jesus in Luke 18: 1-8 provides an analysis of prayer that is social justice and activist-oriented. Between these two events, he presents in the form of a parable a picture of justice as defined and administered in the world. The judge is an embodiment of secular and worldly justice.

Between the judge and God is the poor widow who is culturally susceptible to social biases and prejudices because of her gender and widowhood. She is perhaps about to forfeit her home or her son to a debtor or to be thrown out on the street to become a beggar because of some false allegation. She is weak, desolate, defenseless, and helpless with no powerful friends to call upon. Her only means of intervention and remedy is the available justice system. Jesus presents her as the reason for justice. Her widowhood and poverty not only necessitate justice but also demand the execution of justice as her only means of intervention and vindication. But the judge does not share this view.

First, the judge does not "fear God." Secondly, he does not "care for men." Thirdly, he "neither regards men" and finally, he is simply afraid that the widow's persistence will ruin him and his career: "So she won't eventually wear me out with her coming" (verse 4-5, NIV). He does not want to associate with her and the socio-cultural and economic conditions she represents. He will do all he can to take care of her quickly and from a distance.

In contrast to this judge, God is ready to execute justice for the widow and those she represents. The judge is the custodian of justice in the world, but he is refraining from executing justice for the widow in her desolation. The judge will only execute justice for the widow because it will keep her from bothering him. Furthermore, to intervene on the widow's behalf might enhance his image as a judge and secure his status, secure his personal and family comfort, enhance his reputation for possible advancement in the judicial system or national politics as he contemplates running for public office. He is indifferent, and Jesus calls him an "unjust judge."

To Jesus, the fact that the judge does not fear God, and he has no regard for humanity implies that he does not recognize that justice is Divine. Because he does not recognize that justice is divine, he refuses to objectively execute justice as the inherent right of the "most disadvantaged." For him, justice as "free and equal" for every human being for whom the "fair-terms" of justice at most seeks to "satisfy" in the society is circumspect and qualified.[265] He relies upon the sociopolitical construction of justice that is often historically informed by tribal, cultural, racial, factional interests and stereotypes. He does not acknowledge that justice is divine and ontological.

Jesus is analyzing the existential angst of injustice. As divine, justice is symbolic of the nature of God. In several places in the Old Testament, God is the God of justice, a just and righteous judge. Justice is primarily divine because it has an ontological foundation. The judge does not understand this notion of justice since he does not fear God. He resists justice as divine because an ontological understanding of justice easily convicts his sense of consciousness and seeks to reshape his prejudiced understanding of justice. This socio-culturally construed notion of justice provides eyes, feet, and hands for justice. True justice for him is not blind. In contrast, justice as divine is blind, pure and impartial. It transcends a racially, tribally and culturally defined notion of justice. This judge distorts justice as the spirit of social harmony. He defiles justice as the source of creative unity and destroys justice as the ethos of human mutuality. Justice as the sublime in human relationships is discarded and made secondary for material and sensual reasons.[266]

The judge does not fear God, and secondly, he does not regard men nor care for humanity. He is narcissistic and solipsistic in his administration and execution of justice. He does not care or regard

---

[265] John Rawls, *Justice as Fairness: A Restatement* (New Delhi, Universal, Low Publishing Co. Pvt. Ltd. 2001).

[266] Ibid.,

other human beings and their existential concerns. As a narcissist, he takes pride in his accomplishments and disregards the needs of others. He represents the beautiful youth who is enamored by his beauty; he craves himself and his comfort. As a solipsist, he exists for himself and nothing else. His experience and social location alone provide the paradigm for life.

What a pathetic experience to stand in front of a judge who hates God, hates other human beings and is in love with himself and himself alone. He does not understand nor desire to understand the pain of others except his own.

He holds the view that "only I exist." Everything external to me depends on upon my existence. The existence of the external world is secondary. He portrays the traits of a typical solipsist: "Only my pain is real." The solipsist claims his or her experience is the only "real" experience. "When anything is seen, it is always I who sees it."[267] He cares and identifies only with those who are part of his experience. This interpretation of justice leads to marginalization and alienation of others while members of his circle ravish in the privilege and power associated with his experience.

According to Jesus, the judge is intolerant towards the widow. Her plight does not affect him, except her physical presence, which is a nuisance to him. What about her pain, her tears, and the agony she must bear because of her socio-cultural and economic situation, and the fact that if he does not intervene, she might end up on the street as a beggar or something worst? He refuses to recognize the fact that she is a widow in a society that sees widows as burdensome to the deceased husband's family. Jesus calls him an "unjust" judge. He is a judge, but he is an unjust judge. Any form of justice that suffers from partiality, prejudice, and distortion to the level of disregarding the dignity of a person in Jesus' view is unjust.

Justice must overcome injustice because justice is divine, and injustice is ungodly. Injustice negates the ontological being of any person; it seeks to destroy the inherent dignity of a person and

---

[267] Ludwig Wittgenstein, *Blue and Brown Books* (USA, Harper and Row Publishers, 1958) PP. 57, 61, 63, 64.

reduces him/her to material and corporeal objects; objects that can be commodified, used, abused, misused, and eventually discarded. Injustice is painful because justice is divine. That is why the most uneducated and illiterate man or woman knows what is just and can identify injustice. The spirit of justice is intuitively known, and the spirit of injustice is intuitively known because justice is innate.

Jesus begins the parable with the call to pray and ends the parable with the need to have faith in prayer. I call this praying proactive praying.

Proactive prayer:

The religion is any activity pursued in behalf of an ideal end against obstacles and in spite of threats of personal loss because of its general and enduring value.
(John Dewey).

- The desire to see the tangible and realistic transformation in the dismantling of mass incarceration.
- Action to see the holistic transformation in the lives of those incarcerated that will lead to a decline in the high rate of recidivism.
- A means to achieve objective and impartial justice in three forms of engagements.

Firstly: Proactive Prayer is Transformative Engagement:
- **Transformative Engagement**: Calls upon the Church to raise its voice against the sexual abuses and other forms of brutality perpetrated, especially by correctional officers, and an end to the incarceration and shackling of pregnant women in the United States prison system.

151

- **Transformative Engagement** compels the Church to call for an investigation into the three-strikes sentencing laws across the nation. Based on various reports, three-strikes-you-are-out sentences perpetually target minority men, women and youth, and sentence them to 25 years in jail to support the prison industrial complex.
- **Transformative Engagement** compels the Church to call for an investigation into the policies and practices defining the War-on-Drugs.
- **Transformative Engagement** compels the Church to call for an investigation into the activities of private prisons across the nation the- activities of the commercial prison—industrial complex. The economic emphasis of the commercial prison—industrial complex with its prison stocks on Wall Street having a grave and destructive impact, especially on minority families and communities across the United States.

Secondly: Proactive Prayer is Transparent Engagement.

- **Transparent Engagement** critiques the silence and cognitive dissonance reflected in the attitude of the Church and the American society concerning the destructive implications of mass incarceration.
- **Transparent Engagement** calls upon the Church to appeal to the democratic principles of the United States and its Constitution to demand transformation in the sentencing policies and prison reform across the United States.
- **Transparent Engagement** calls upon the Church to raise its voice in critiquing those structures and institutions that undermine human flourishing, justice, fairness, and equality in the criminal justice system.

Thirdly: Proactive Prayer is Transcendent Engagement.

- **Transcendent Engagement** appeals to the concept of justice as divine and ontological.
- **Transcendent Engagement** appeals to the concept of impartial justice as fundamental to the sentencing process.
- **Transcendent Engagement** argues for the respect and recognition of human dignity in the sentencing process and the American prison system in light of the high rates of human abuse and violation of human rights in the United States prison system.

For Jesus, justice is divine. Justice as divine pushes us to the edge to look within, ask the hard questions and embark upon the difficult actions. To implement justice is to execute a divine mandate for the common good and the flourishing of humanity.

A Critical Response

Unless theology can become 'ghetto theology,' a theology which speaks to black people, the gospel message has no promise of life for the black man- it is a lifeless message.
(James Cone –*Black Theology & Black Power* p. 32).

A critical response is an introspective analysis of the Black community. To look in the mirror and put one's house in order is the best approach to strategic solution development. A critical response demands that we assume responsibilities for those things we have done, measures we have failed to take that have contributed to the present demise of the Black community. While we do agree that there are overshadowing historical and socio-political factors responsible for mass Black incarceration and detention, we must also acknowledge the fact that there are individual factors that have contributed and are still contributing to mass Black incarceration.

As a result of American individualism, consumerism coupled with sociopolitical and economic racism and alienation, intra-Black marginalization and alienation have given rise to several negative issues in the community. Also, the refusal to adopt the practice of "intergenerational-communication" has engendered a sociocultural and religious isolation for the present generation of Black youths.

What is "intergenerational-communication"? It is the passing on of narratives and experiences from one generation to another for self-preservation and instruction. Every tribe, race, nation, community, village, and clan fights to preserve its struggles, accomplishments, and aspirations to pass onto the next generation as substantial legacies for self-propagation. But this generation of Black men, women, and youth caught in the tentacles of mass Black incarceration is symptomatic of grave community and family fragmentation reflected in intra-Black alienation and isolation. It is in this light that the preacher in the Black community, the Black leader, the Black intellectual, and the Black parent must understand their role as continuous with the historical responsibility to instruct this generation. The pulpit must be employed to instruct; the dinner table must be transformed into a mini classroom while the television and computer perceived as tools to push this generation into the ever-increasing technological age. Mass Black incarceration robs the Black community of its intellectual capital, its sociopolitical and economic resources, all reflected in human potential, dreams, and aspirations. Mass Black incarceration is a systemic destruction of the Black family, the Black community, and Black intellectual advancement. The highest number of Black men incarcerated are between the ages of 20-39, a period characteristic of the blossoming of intellectual, spiritual, artistic, sociopolitical and economic strength and virtues of the community.

Unfortunately, the abundance of intellectual capital sentenced to long-term incarceration in America's prisons reflects America's intellectual capital, languishing in prisons, jails and detention camps across the nation.

The critical response calls upon Black ministers, community leaders, and parents to pay careful attention to what is happening to this present generation of Black men and women. We are faced with the potential scarcity of Black men to uphold the Black family structure in America. With over 3 million Black men, women, and youths in detention camps, juvenile facilities, prisons, on parole, probation or under some form of correctional supervision, the numbers of the future leaders and custodians of the Black community and family structures continue to diminish. With poor quality education and a poorly resourced public school system in Black communities across the United States, attention should also be drawn to the pervasiveness of thug-life as a major challenge to urban Black youths. Per Kenneth D. Johnson, the socioeconomic and political impacts on the future of Black youths are regrettable. He argues that

> Structural changes in the economy demanding higher levels of education as the minimum passport for entry to gainful employment has left a generation of youths and young male adults behind . . . Due to broken families . . . increasingly young urban families yield themselves to negative male peer influences in a desperate search for identity, security, and instruction on how to survive and get one's needs met in a hostile society. The previous buffering effects of the trinity of home, school and church have been dissolved, with none of these institutions offering credible and engaging alternative lifestyle on a consistent basis that meets youth's needs for material security and advancement and to satisfy their need to belong to something greater than themselves. Thug life offers youths a seductive, but ultimately self-defeating set of choices that eventually result in harm.[268]

An important area to address because of mass Black incarceration is the prevailing HIV/AIDS epidemic in the Black community. To advocate for the use of condoms may seem to encourage sex between inmates. However, the need to quell the spread of HIV/AIDS in the Black community as a direct result

---

[268] *Antioch Agenda: Essays on the Restorative Church in Honor of Orlando E. Costas*, 2007, 214.

of mass Black incarceration and detention cannot be dismissed. According to Eli Coleman, professor, and director of the Program in Human Sexuality at the University of Minnesota Medical School, "whether legal or not, sex between inmates is occurring, and we must do what we can to provide vehicles for responsible sexual behavior, including the use of condoms."[269] In addition to the spread of HIV/AIDS as a direct result of mass Black incarceration, the rate of mental health and suicide cases has increased in the Black community. Several factors including the sociopolitical and economic factors are intricately related to the implications of mass Black incarceration.

> *My people are destroyed for lack of knowledge.*
> Hosea 4:6a

> *Our lives begin to end the day we become silent about things that matter.*
> Martin Luther King, Jr.

Mental Health, Suicide and Mass Black Incarceration:

> **Prisons are bad for mental health:** There are factors in many prisons that have negative effects on mental health, including: overcrowding, various forms of violence, enforced solitude, or conversely, lack of privacy, lack of meaningful activity, isolation from social networks, insecurity about future prospects (work, relationships, etc.), and inadequate health services, especially mental health services, in prisons. The increased risk of suicide in prisons (often related to depression) is, unfortunately, one common manifestation of the cumulative

---

[269] Dan Childs: *Free Condoms for Prisoners?: Barrier Contraception Could Stem High Level of HIV Infection in Correctional Facilities.* http://abcnews.go.com/print?id=2724605

effects of these factors (World Health Organization-*Mental Health and Prisons*).[270]

The United States prison system has a high rate of incarceration of individuals with mental health issues.[271] According to the Treatment Advocacy Center for May 2010 report: *More Mentally Ill Persons are in Jails and Prisons than Hospitals: A Survey of States*:

> Recent studies suggest that at least 16 percent of inmates in jails and prisons have a serious mental illness. In 1983 a similar study reported that the percentage was 6.4 percent. Thus, in less than three decades, the percentage of seriously mentally ill prisoners has almost tripled.[272]

Because of mass Black Incarceration, mental health, and suicide cases have increased in the Black community. According to the

---

[270] World Health Organization: *Mental Health and Prisons*. "Mental disorders occur at high rates in all countries of the world. An estimated 450 million people worldwide suffer from mental or behavioural disorders. These disorders are especially prevalent in prison populations. The disproportionately high rate of mental disorders in prisons is related to several factors: the widespread misconception that all people with mental disorders are a danger to the public; the general intolerance of many societies to difficult or disturbing behaviour; the failure to promote treatment, care and rehabilitation, and, above all, the lack of, or poor access to, mental health services in many countries. Many of these disorders may be present before admission to prison, and may be further exacerbated by the stress of imprisonment. However, mental disorders may also develop during imprisonment itself as a consequence of prevailing conditions and also possibly due to torture or other human rights violations." (http://www.who.int/mental_health/policy/mh_in_prison.pdf)

[271] Bureau of Justice Statistics Special Report: *Mental Health Problems of Prisons and Jails Inmates*. "At midyear 2005 more than half of all prison and jail inmates had a mental health problem, including 705,600 inmates in State prisons, 78,800 in Federal prisons, and 479,900 in local jails. These estimates represented 56% of State prisoners, 45% of Federal prisoners, and 64% of jail inmates. The findings in this report were based on data from personal interviews with State and Federal prisoners in 2004 and local jail inmates in 2002." (http://bjs.ojp.usdoj.gov/content/pub/pdf/mhppji.pdf)

[272] Treatment Advocacy Center: *More Mentally Ill Persons are in Jails and Prisons than Hospitals: A Survey of States*. http://www.treatmentadvocacycenter.org/storage/documents/final_jails_v_hospitals_study.pdf

studies: *Souls of Black Men: African American Men Discuss Mental Health*:

- 7% of African American men will develop depression during their lifetime. This is likely to be an underestimate due to lack of screening and treatment services.
- African American men have death rates that are at least twice as high as those of women for suicide, cirrhosis of the liver, and homicide.

- From 1980 to 1995, the suicide rate for African-American male youth (ages 15-19) increased by 146%.
- Among African American males aged 15-19 years; firearms were used in 72% of suicides, while strangulation was used in 20% of suicides.[273]

While several studies have highlighted the link between racism and mental health issues for Blacks in America, the link between mass Black incarceration and the increase in Black mental health/suicide rates has not received much attention. The long-term implications for the Black community are grave and merely accidental. They are structural, medical and existential issues that deserve maximum attention. The mental health issues affecting Black women are becoming increasingly severe. Alternatives to incarceration must be considered in developing strategic solutions to remedy the situation.[274] According to the

---

[273] *Souls of Black Men: African American Men Discuss Mental Health*: http://www.consumerstar.org/pubs/Souls.pdf

[274] D. Erika Kates: *Exploring Alternative to Incarceration* (ATI) for Women in Massachusetts: "There are multiple definitions of diversion practices – from pre-arrest practices or 'front end' diversion to post-incarceration practices, or "back-end" measures. A review of ATI practices involves a complex and diverse mix of agencies, expertise, and goals. Pre-arrest and pre-arraignment diversion – refers people exhibiting mental distress or disorderly behavior to clinical programs for assessment and treatment rather than arrest. Pre-trial diversion or intervention; deferred prosecution or disposition before judgment – after a detailed assessment a person is referred to community-based resources or is given a suspended sentences. Probation, community corrections, alternative dispositions, intermediate sanctions and accelerated rehabilitative disposition -- allows offenders to remain in the community

report: *Health Issues in the Black Community* edited by Ronald L. Braithwaite, Sandrae E. Taylor, and Henrie M. Treadwell:

> The multiple health issues of incarcerated women including addictive sexual and reproductive health as well as serious and chronic mental and physical conditions, cannot be omitted from any discussion of prison life...The disproportion of incarcerated black women is reflected in statistics that show black women to be seven times more likely to be incarcerated in their lifetime than white women and two times more likely than Hispanic women. The health of this population differs significantly from women in the general population and is a price paid not only by the inmates themselves but also by the inmate's children, who are often left with a plethora of complexities with which to deal.[275]

The report: *Souls of Black Men* argues that the high rate of mental health issues and suicide prevalent among Black men are attributed to factors that include racism, poverty, and economic inequalities, depression and a debilitating sense of rejection in America, especially for Black men from poor backgrounds. It argues that:

- When mental disorders aren't treated, African American men are more vulnerable to incarceration, homelessness, substance abuse, homicide, and suicide.
- Poverty, racism and the impact of past trauma (particularly violence) are the primary contributing factors to the mental health disorders of young African American men.
- Young blacks are more likely to commit suicide after an altercation or perceived victimization by institutional authorities

---

while under the supervision of the courts, usually under the auspices of probation. Incarceration, prison and jail are included in a review of alternatives to incarceration because imprisonment may be a joint sentence with probation and parole. Also, prerelease programs are regarded as essential in efforts to reduce recidivism."
(http://www.wcwonline.org/pdf/ekates/ATISummary9.11.pdf)
[275] *Health Issues in the Black Community*. http://www.scribd.com/doc/26450232/Health-Issues-in-the-Black-Community

such as the police, criminal justice system, school officials, landlords or welfare departments.[276]

Consequences of Mass Black Incarceration for the Black Community:

- Increase in HIV/AIDS in the Black community.
- The decline in eligible Black men for marriage.
- The breakdown of the family structure.
- Increase in Black women infected with HIV/AIDS.
- Increase in the incarceration of Black women.
- Increase in psycho-social and mental health problems.
- Increase in Black suicide rates because of socio-cultural and economic marginalization from mainstream America, associated with mass Black incarceration.

He who passively accepts evil is as much involved in it as he who helps to perpetrate it. He who accepts evil without protesting it is really cooperating with it.

(Martin Luther King, Jr.).

---

[276] *Souls of Black Men: African American Men Discuss Mental Health.* "More than one in four adults experience a mental health or substance abuse disorder in any given year. Yet only a small percentage of those affected will be properly diagnosed and treated for their disorder. For African American men and their families, the consequences of neglected mental health needs are devastating – Prevention: Early intervention is critical. Outreach must be tailored specifically for African American men and health education must be delivered by trusted messengers. Develop and support mental health promotion/intervention initiatives that are specifically geared to African American males. Develop early intervention strategies for men who are vulnerable to environmental and psychosocial factors that predispose them to self-destructive behaviors. Suicide prevention efforts should be evidence-based and comprehensive enough to address the complex dynamics of suicidal behaviors." http://www.consumerstar.org/pubs/Souls.pdf

A Rational Response

The U.S Department of Justice estimates that 16% of the adult inmates in American prisons and jails-which means more than 350,000 of those locked up-suffer from mental illness, and the percentage in juvenile custody is even higher. Our correctional institutions are also heavily populated by the 'criminally ill,' including inmates who suffer from HIV/AIDS, tuberculosis, and hepatitis.

(Senator Jim Webb, *What's wrong With Our Prisons?* Boston Sunday Globe Parade, pp.4-5).

A rational response is a social justice response. It is a solution-oriented response that looks at how activists and leaders fought against the inhumane incarceration of other human beings in human history.

According to King, the scarred souls, the emotional angst of racial suspicion and criminalization, the existential toil of family breakups from slavery to mass Black incarceration, and the dilemma of being Black require strategic intervention and healing. He writes:

> The Negro cannot constructively deal with his dilemma through negative strategies. In spite of uncertainties and vicissitudes we must develop the courage to confront the negatives of circumstance with the positives of inner determination.[277]

---

[277] King, 1968, p. 122

King provides a list of "positive responses":

The development of a "rugged sense of somebodyness."[278]

To overcome the ravages of the past, the Black person will have to stop seeing themselves as worthless to cultivating a "majestic sense of worth", the "chains of an oppressive society" can no longer be tolerated to "shackle our minds."[279] A daring sense of self-worth must be cultivated to "stabilize our egos" and to provide the expected "confirmation of our roots and a validation of our worth."[280]

The refusal to be ashamed of one's Blackness:

"Life's piano can only produce the melodies of brotherhood when it is recognized that the black keys are as basic, necessary and beautiful as the white keys." The Black person, he explains must endure the process of "self-acceptance" and "self-appreciation" to exercise their God-given talents, gifts, and skills. [281]

The development of mental power to overcome the objectification of the past.

It takes "courage" and "determination" to overthrow the debilitations of the past to arrive at the fountain of self-respect, self-confidence, and self-acceptance.[282]

The development of a sense of "group identity":

King distinguishes group identity from "group isolation" or "group exclusivity." [283] Group identity flourishes on the principles of the group-reconciliation, group trust, and group

---

[278] King, 1968, p. 122
[279] King, 1968, p. 122
[280] King, 1968, p. 123
[281] King, 1968, p. 123.
[282] King, 1968, p. 123.
[283] King, 1968, p. 125.

restoration. It entails respect for self and respect for others. According to King,

> Too many Negroes are jealous of other Negroes' success and progress. Too many Negro organizations are warring against each other with a claim to absolute truth. The Pharaohs had a favorite and effective strategy to keep their slaves in bondage: keep them fighting among themselves. The divide-and-conquer techniques has been a potent weapon in the arsenal of oppression. But when slaves unite, the Red Seas of history open and the Egypts of slavery crumble.[284]

Furthermore, group identity does not imply group uniformity. Group identity also flourishes on "healthy debate" and exchange of ideas. In this respect, King suggests:

> There are already structured forces in the Negro community that can serve as the basis for building a powerful united front-the Negro church, the Negro press... This form of group unity can do infinitely more to liberate the Negro than any action of individuals. We have been oppressed as a group and we must overcome that oppression as a group. [285]

The development of group force to overthrow the "last vestiges of racial injustice."[286]

This process requires what King refers to as "mass nonviolent action" through the ballot box. It is an effective strategy to advocate for equality in opportunities for education, jobs, housing, representation, and inclusion. He warns:

---

[284] King, 1968, p. 124
[285] King, 1968, pp. 124-5.
[286] King, 1968, p. 128

> The relatively privileged Negro will never be
> what he ought to be until the underprivileged
> Negro is what he ought to be. The salvation of
> the Negro middle class is ultimately dependent
> upon the salvation of the Negro masses.[287]

In the eighteenth century, prisons in England were filthy, dingy and disease-ridden. While these conditions may slightly differ from the mass incarceration of human beings existing in the United States' prison system in the 21st century, the abject caging and dehumanization of human beings associated with large-scale incarceration remains the same.

John Wesley started a prison ministry in 1730 as part of his Oxford Methodists ministry. Wesley established his concept of ministry on his understanding of the teaching of Jesus in Matthew 25:31-46. He directed his ministry to help the poor and disadvantaged. It included visitation together with the sharing of the gospel message with the hope that transformation will take place in the heart of the prisoners. Prisons in this era were dirty, dingy, and unsanitary. Prisoners were surviving on small meals and the lack of medical attention. Prison conditions were often unfavorable. Most of the diseases were contagious. Sarah Peters, a ministry colleague of Wesley, became exposed to what was called "jail fever" and died.

According to Wesley's Journal, he preached to forty-seven prisoners on death row at Newgate on December 26, 1784. Ludgage and Newgate prisons in London were found to be in terrible shape and were condemned by Wesley. One Mr. William Morgan introduced Wesley to the prisons. He writes,

> In the summer following, Mr. Morgan told me he had called...to
> see a man that was condemned for killing his wife, and that from
> the talk he had with one of his debtors he verily believed that it
> would do much good if anyone would be at the pains now and

---

[287] King, 1968, p. 132

then of speaking with them. This he so frequently repeated that on the 24th of August, 1730, my brother and I walked down with him to the Castle. We were so well satisfied with our conversation there that we agreed to go thither once or twice a week.[288]

These visits marked the beginning of Wesley's prison ministry as final ecclesiastical approval came from the bishop of Oxford's chaplain, Mr. Gerard. With his foundational text, Matt. 25: 31-46, Wesley and his colleagues could solicit funding for the ministry. Though it was a bit difficult, the Oxford Methodists as they later called themselves were eventually able to get the ministry off the ground and running. But they had to get approval from every town through the advice of one Rev. Joseph Hoole, the vicar of Haxey.[289] Recorded in his diary on Monday, October 15, Wesley expanded his ministry activities to a prison that held French prisoners at Knowle. He writes,

> I walked up to Knowle, a mile from Bristol, to see the French prisoners. About eleven hundred of them, we were informed, were confined in that little place without anything to lie on but a little dirty straw, or anything to cover them but a few foul thin rags, either by day or night, so that they died like rotten sheep. I was much affected, and preached in the evening on Exodus 23: 9— 'Thou shall not oppress a stranger; for ye know the heart of a stranger, seeing ye were strangers in the land of Egypt. Eighteen pounds were contributed immediately, which were made up [to] four and twenty the next day. With this, we bought linen and woolen cloth, which were made up into shirts, waistcoats, and breeches.[290]

For Wesley, immigrants in prisons were no different from citizens in prisons; both groups were exposed to the same treatment.

---

[288] John Wesley: *The Works of John Wesley*, Eds. Richard Heitzenrater, W. Reginald Ward, *The Bicentennial Edition, Vol. 19* (Nashville, Tennessee: Abingdon Press, 1990), 25: 337.

[289] Ibid., 25: 341-342

[290] Ibid., 21: 285

Not only was he concerned about clothing and feeding prisoners, but Wesley was also equally concerned about their education. On August 1, 1732, Wesley got a letter from a fellow Oxford Methodist about the reading ability of two prisoners.[291] But not everyone approved of Wesley's prison ministry. Opposition came from those who thought his work was an infringement and a nuisance.

Wesley's prison activities, like his ardent condemnation of the institution of slavery, emerged because of his salvation experience and the fact that the gospel of Jesus was holistic in its appeal to human estrangement from God and self. It was experiences like these that helped Wesley to formulate his holistic understanding of the gospel of Jesus into what he called "Scriptural holiness" and "Social holiness." Both scriptural holiness and social holiness underscore the understanding that salvation and renewal in Christ Jesus were the fundamental inspiration for social action. While social actions have their positive influences, they tend to be strictly secularized. The limitation of a secularized mode of social action in this context is its lack of emphasis on conversion and transformation. Wesley believed scriptural holiness informs social holiness in its social activities. Social justice and engagement in the struggle were not incompatible to preaching the gospel of Jesus Christ.[292]

Wesley believed the structural transformation in the criminal justice system could only be possible if raised to the level of public awareness and institutional consciousness. This conviction in Wesley was evident in his concern for prison reform and the criminal justice system of England. Wesley was adamant that the criminal justice system of England at the time needed to open its

---

[291] Richard P. Heitzenrater, *The Bicentennial Edition, vol. 21* (Nashville, Tennessee: Abingdon Press, 1992,) 25: 331-334. "Two of the felons likewise have paid their fees and gone out, both of them able to read might well. John Clanville, who reads but moderately, and the horse-dealer, who cannot read at all. He knows all his letters and can spell most of the common monosyllables. I hear them both read three times a week . . ."

[292] Ronald Stone, *John Wesley's Life & Ethics* (Nashville, Abingdon Press 2001).

eyes to the horrible conditions associated with English prisons. For Wesley, it was a grave condemnation:

> O England, England! Will this reproach never be rolled away from thee? Is there anything like this to be found either among Papists, Turks, or heathens? In the name of truth, justice, mercy, and common sense, I ask . . .[293]

Wesley eventually made prison visitation mandatory for all Methodist
Preachers. God instructed him to address the conditions of prisoners in the English prison system, and he felt it was necessary for all ministers to observe the same instruction.[294] Wesley was affected by the shared sense of human mutuality, regardless of race, class, education, nationality, etc. Given the above, a rational response asserts the claim for a second chance for prisoners.

According to the Gospels, Jesus fed the hungry, conversed with the Samaritan woman, raised Lazarus from the dead, delivered the demon-possessed man, fed five thousand people, healed the woman with the issue of blood, turned the tables upside down in the temple, and rebuked the members of the Sanhedrin Council for their

---

[293] In Donald Henry Kirkham's *"Pamphlet Opposition to the Rise of Methodism: The Eighteenth-Century English Evangelical Revival Under Attack,"* (PhD, diss., Duke University, 1973, p. 202) 21: 333

[294] According to Rev. Brad Thie, "From the beginning, ministry to prisoners was part of the established repertoire of Methodist activity. In 1778 it was confirmed by a Conference decision and made obligatory for all preachers."— "Wesley's prison ministry belies his being 'tenacious of every point relating to decency.' He continuously ministered despite opposition from theological opponents, irritation form turnkeys, and the threat of serious disease and death. He courageously entered the penal system at a time when it was not fashionable to do so either theologically or socially. He did so consistently, and upheld the vitality of prison ministry in the Rules of the United Societies and in 'The Character of a Methodist.' Whether we label his social ethics a virtue or obligation ethic, or both, Wesley consistently nurtured this vital ministry that his friend William Morgan introduced him to in the summer of 1730. The prison ministry, for Wesley, was a critical focus for those who called themselves Methodists, lay and clergy alike. To continue to minister, and to be ministered to in prison settings, is an action congruent with reclaiming the rich heritage given to us by those who first called themselves Methodists." Brad Thie-WNCc-Revised 9/99 (http://gbgm-umc. org/mission_programs/mcr/4.35/theprison.cfm)

self-interest brand of leadership, and their distortion of the Word of God. Based on what Jesus did, especially actions that negated the traditional perception, we find no distinction between what was spiritual and what was social. A rational response challenges the nature of our message and ministry.

The tendency to uncritically subscribe to the "prosperity" message is problematic in this regard. Preaching prosperity without a sociopolitical and economic analysis is like preaching the Gospel of Jesus and avoiding the passages about Jesus ridding the temple of money changers, get-rich-quick preaching, and preachers, racism in the Church, unscrupulous loan agents, etc. The logic of the prosperity message can be reduced to the following: if you are poor, it's because you have sinned or are living in sin; if you are rich, it's because God loves you and you are living a holy life. Poverty and the poor are associated with immorality and incontinence while wealth and the wealthy are associated with holiness and morality. Because of this understanding, we excuse ourselves from helping and taking the initiative to help the poor, the marginalized and disenfranchised since it is their fault. While I do believe the biblical injunction that the "wages of sin is death" (Romans 6:23), I also believe that there are social factors responsible for poverty and economic disparities. It is called "social sin" according to Walters Rauschenbusch. The prosperity message in its unqualified form distorts the nature of God because it becomes overbearingly judgmental and guilt-ridden. If we biblically and logically analyze the argument for the popular prosperity teaching, we may conclude that the victims of mass Black incarceration in the United States are the worst sinners in the world. While there are some who deserve to be incarcerated, there is a multitude of them who were arbitrarily and unjustly arrested, and incarcerated. Arrest, detention, and incarceration are also carried out to make up the detention and incarceration statistics, the gathering of quotas for the support of the commercial prison—industrial complex, and to keep the momentum of public safety in the eyes of the public. A proper elaboration of the prosperity message should reflect the preacher's desire to help those who are poor, sick, imprisoned, and widowed. Let them experience prosperity and not condemnation. The Body of Christ and the Black community now need a holistic approach to dismantling mass incarceration defined within the context of:

> *I believe in Liberty for all men: the space to stretch their arms and their souls; the right to breathe and the right to vote, the freedom to choose their friends, enjoy the sunshine, and ride on the railroads, by color; thinking, dreaming, working as they will in a kingdom of beauty and love.*
> (W.E.B. Du Bois).

- **Respect** for human dignity in the United States, criminal justice, and prison systems, etc. Investigating the profiling and targeting of minority men, women and youths to support mass Black incarceration.
- **Reform:** in the sentencing process including Three-strikes laws, mandatory minimums: longer, and punitive sentencing measures especially for the most non-violent crimes.
- **Rehabilitation:** of prisoners with an intentional emphasis on program development, skills development, and preparation for employment.
- **Restoration**: the involvement of religious, civic and reentry institutions together with family support groups to help facilitate the less strenuous reintegration of formerly incarcerated individuals with the goal to reduce the high rate of recidivism.

The rational response is a humanitarian critique of the American prison and criminal justice systems.

A Pragmatic Response

*The underprivileged everywhere have long since abandoned any
hope that this type of salvation deals with the crucial issues by
which their days are turned into despair without consolation.*
(Howard Thurman, *Jesus and the Disinherited,* p. 29).

Mass incarceration in the United States is a humanitarian crisis. A pragmatic response is a tangible, realistic and commonsense approach to dismantling mass incarceration in the United States. Human rights violations and abuses in the United States' prison system because of mass incarceration necessitate a decisive condemnation from humanitarian and religious bodies. Their implications are grave and existential. This decisive condemnation calls for investigation into the war on drugs waged since 1971 and the sentencing policies associated with it. This "War" has cost billions of dollars while simultaneously distorting lives, breaking up families, destroying human potential, ingenuity, and aspirations, especially of those accused of non-violent offenses. Sadly, the major targets of the war on drugs are Blacks, Hispanics, and poor Whites with Black men, women, and juveniles accounting for the highest group of individuals caught in the American criminal justice system.

Blacks and Hispanics are over 65% of those behind bars and under some form of correctional supervision. Black men are close to 45% of those behind bars, and Black women have the highest rate of female incarceration in the United States three times higher than their Hispanic and White counterparts. Also, Black juveniles consist of the highest group of children detained in the United States' juvenile detention facilities. Blacks are 12-13% of the entire population of the United States, thus the phrase: "Mass Black Incarceration."

The existential implications of mass Black incarceration are reflected in:

- An increase in fatherlessness and single parenting in the Black community.
- A breakdown in the Black family structure.
- The lack of economic mobility for most Black men/women and juveniles because of felony or conviction records.
- An increase in poverty and intergenerational impoverishment.
- An increase in the HIV/AIDS epidemic in the Black community as a result of longer, and punitive sentences for Blacks in the United States' prison system.
- An increase in mental health disorders and suicide for Blacks due to marginalization, stigmatization, isolation, and the augmentation of mass Black incarceration.

It is the argument of this book that the offender is not an inherent criminal. Every mitigating factor pertinent to the case must be taken into consideration because every human being has the potential to be rehabilitated. While we do not condone egregious crimes against other human beings, we are certainly hopeful that change is possible in the life of the offender. This position contrasts with the retributive argument of Hegel on crime and punishment as analyzed throughout this book. His perspective on crime and punishment criminalizes the offender for the rest of his or her life and closes the door to any form of rehabilitation. Inherent criminality disregards all mitigating factors in the adjudication of a case except for those that enhance the case of the prosecutor. The argument that "once a criminal always a criminal." According to the report: *Prisoner, Reentry, Religion, and Research,*

> Since the beginning of prisons and jails, religion has influenced philosophies of punishment and rehabilitation. Whether motivated by religious beliefs or a sense of civic

171

duty, "the church" has helped direct the course of modern corrections. For more than a century, the church has been relied upon to provide spiritual guidance and support to prisoners. The church has also provided and continues to provide, a wider range of secular services to prisoners, ex-prisoners, and their families.[295]

This final section of the book argues for the development of strategic solution towards to dismantle the structures of mass incarceration considering the influence of religion/faith. Religious conversion and religious institutions have been researched to reduce recidivism, infractions, and repeated offenses in the life of the offender. The life of Malcolm X attests to the transformative power of religion as a viable and reliable experience in reducing recidivism. He explains this 1948 religious epiphany from Norfolk Prison in Massachusetts.

> I remember how, sometime later, reading the Bible in the Norfolk Prison Colony library, I came upon, then I read, over and over, how Paul on the road to Damascus, upon hearing the voice of Christ, was so smitten that he was knocked off his horse, in a daze. I do not now, and I did not then, liken myself to Paul. But I do understand his experience. I have since learned–helping me to understand what then began to happen within me-that the truth can be quickly received, or received at all, only by the sinner who knows and admits that he is guilty of having sinned much. Stated another way: only guilt admitted accepts truth. The Bible again: the one people

---

[295] *Prisoner Reentry Religion, and Research.* "The historic role of the Church combined with its potential for volunteer resources uniquely position the faith community to support the successful reintegration of returning prisoners. While the church…Religious measures were generally inversely related to juvenile delinquency in the 13 studies that used reliability testing of religious measures. These findings also show that religiosity had a negative effect on deviance in the most methodologically rigorous studies. While many of the studies did not use random sampling, multiple indicators to control measurement errors, or reliability testing of their measures, the higher-quality studies generally found a negative relationship between religiosity and delinquency." https://peerta.acf.hhs.gov/pdf/prisoner_reentry.pdf

whom Jesus could not help were the Pharisees; they didn't feel they needed any help.[296]

Malcolm converted to the Nation of Islam in 1952. The Nation of Islam has consistently reached out to inmates and has contributed immensely to rehabilitating many inmates and preparing them for re-entry and adequate re-integration into the community. The research further concludes that:

> The faith community, however, is perhaps a partner in prisoner reentry and is uniquely positioned to provide a variety of services to support the successful re-integration of returning prisoners. Religious program research may hold a valuable key to developing criminal justice system solutions.[297]

The role of religious institutions in dismantling mass incarceration is also a synthesis of sociopolitical action and spiritual responsibilities at the same time rehabilitating and restoring the offender. The goal is to transform policies and laws enacted to perpetuate mass incarceration and its systemic means of profiteering at the expense of crime and punishment. Emphasis on rehabilitation must be paramount to the process of criminal justice reform. While religion is a partner in the process of dismantling mass incarceration, it is important to state that the success of religion/faith can only be long lasting if combined with a rigorous process of prison reform. Penal transformation is possible if religious institutions raise their voice to influence and inform public policies and sentencing laws. Mass incarceration is also made possible with the passing of sentencing laws like three-strikes and mandatory minimums in California, which had a rippling effect across the United States.

---

[296] Alex Haley: *The Autobiography of Malcolm X* (New York, Ballantine Books, 1964), Pp.166-167.

[297] Ibid. https://peerta.acf.hhs.gov/pdf/prisoner_reentry.pdf: "The aforementioned findings suggest that faith is the forgotten factor in reducing crime problems and religious program research may hold a valuable key to developing criminal justice system solution."

These laws were adopted by several states with Massachusetts as the latest to do so in 2012. Similarly, the process of dismantling mass incarceration and the injustices associated with mass Black incarceration require intentional efforts and engagement. I argue in this book that mass incarceration is inherently anti-justice, that it militates against human flourishing, and it distorts human dignity.

Whoever sets any bounds for the reconstructive power of the religious life over the social relations and institutions of men, to that extent denies the faith of the Master.
(Walter Rauschenbusch).

The following initiatives are suggested towards dismantling mass incarceration, or better said: mass Black incarceration in the United States.

1. Communicate with your children:

Tell your children and your youth department members about the dangers of going to prison. Tell them: With a criminal record they will experience economic hardship: it will be difficult to find employment, difficult to get a loan for college, almost impossible to purchase a home, and because of the above, it will be almost impossible to properly take care of a family. And these hardships are to a large extent because of your criminal record. With a criminal record: you will be socially stigmatized and economically marginalized from mainstream society because of your lack of adequate education, joblessness and lack of skills for social mobility. As a result of this social marginalization, you might end up going back to prison. With a criminal record, you are economically disempowered; politically you cannot vote and psychologically you will be very disturbed. Finally, in prison, people easily get infected with HIV/AIDS as a result of consensual and non-consensual sex between inmates than among people on the outside. In prisons, the use of condoms is not mandatory nor are they distributed. It is a hard life to live.

2. The establishment of Faith-based reintegration programs mainly for juvenile ex-offenders:

Faith-based organizations can develop reintegration programs that will make it possible for a smooth transition into the society, especially for juvenile offenders who are constantly in search of security and stability.

3. The establishment of Faith-based programs for job training and job placement:

A Faith-based initiative for job training will make it possible for ex-offenders to get their GED, develop self-confidence, and not be ashamed of themselves. One of the major reasons for the high rate of recidivism among Black men is the lack of education and skills needed for employment. As Bell beautifully articulates in his essay in *The Covenant with Black America*, the goal is "education rather than incarceration." [298] The focus should, therefore, be on improving quality education for Black youths. The link between education and incarceration is reflected in the high rate of recidivism and prior incarceration records. The implication is an increase in the rate of high school dropouts for Black youths if they are not attended to with concerted efforts. Uneducated Black men easily end up in jail because of the lack of skills for employment.

4. The establishment of Faith-based rehabilitation programs that cater to the Black child's sense of consciousness.

Churches can investigate the possibility of preventing Black children from entering the Department of Youth Services (DYS) at the alarming rate at which they have entered this system. The thrust of a Faith-based rehabilitation program is its emphasis on rehabilitation and restoration through religious counseling programs. The goal is to prevent Black youths from becoming perpetual inmates and addicts hooked on prescriptive drugs provided as a result of clinical measures. In this context, faith-

---

[298] *The Covenant With Black America*, 2006, 65

based organizations are called upon to be proactive in employing the transformative understanding of their faith.

5. The establishment of Faith-based Social Justice Ministry:

Every Faith-based organization should endeavor to have a social justice agenda. The goal of this ministry is to inform and engage its members in issues of social concerns affecting the community. It means working in collaboration with other organizations to be conversant and cognizant of the prevailing social conditions of the community.

The church that is serious about adopting the above points among others should know that it is taking a great risk. It will transform the ministry of the church considering its commitment to the gospel of Jesus Christ. The church that wants to commit to the above must find solace in the fact that it is engaged in the proclamation of the pure gospel of Jesus Christ. On the other hand, if a church's focus is amassing wealth and increasing membership without committing itself to the social-existential needs of its members, it is certainly failing to provide a holistic interpretation of the gospel of Jesus Christ in message and in deeds. Silence is the best weapon for normalizing a dangerous situation and insensitivity is its advocate.

Yes, I see the Church as the body of Christ. But, oh! How we have blemished and scarred that body through social neglect and through fear of being nonconformists.

(Martin Luther King, Jr.).

I confess, my God, that I have long been, and even now am, recalcitrant to the love of my neighbor. Just as much as I have derived intense joy in the superhuman delight of dissolving myself and losing myself in the souls for which I was destined by the mysterious affinities of human love, so I have always felt an inborn hostility to, and closed myself to, the common run of those whom you tell me to love. I find no difficulty in integrating into my inward life everything above and beneath me . . . But "the other man," my God—by which I do not mean "the poor, the halt, the lame and the sick," but "the other" quite simply as "other," the one who seems to exist independently of me because his universe seems closed to mine, and who seems to shatter the unity and the silence of the world for me—would I be sincere if I did not confess that my instinctive reaction is to rebuff him? And that the mere thought of entering into spiritual communication with him disgusts me?

Grant, O God that the light of your countenance may shine for me in the life of that "other." The irresistible light of your eyes shining the depth of things has already guided me towards all the work I must accomplish, and all the difficulties I must pass through. Grant that I may see you, even and above all, in the souls of my brothers, at their most personal, and most true, and most distant.

(Pierre Teilhard De Chardin: *The Divine Milieu: An Essay on the Interior Life,* 145-156).

APPENDIX

America Has Lost a Generation of Black Boys

By: Phillip Jackson
Posted March 21, 2007, in the Chattanoogan.Com

There is no longer a need for dire predictions, hand-wringing, or apprehension about losing a generation of Black boys. It is too late. In education, employment, economics, incarceration, health, housing, and parenting, we have lost a generation of young Black men. The question that remains is will we lose the next two or three generations, or possibly every generation of Black boys hereafter to the streets, negative media, gangs, drugs, poor education, unemployment, father absence, crime, violence, and death.

Most young Black men in the United States don't graduate from high school. Only 35% of Black male students graduated from high school in Chicago and only 26% in New York City, according to a 2006 report by The Schott Foundation for Public Education. Only a few Black boys who finish high school actually attend college, and of those few Black boys who enter college, nationally, only 22% of them finish college.

Young Black male students have the worst grades, the lowest test scores, and the highest dropout rates of all students in the country. When these young Black men don't succeed in school, they are much more likely to succeed in the nation's criminal justice and penitentiary systems. And it was discovered recently that even when

179

a young Black man graduates from a U.S. college, there is a good chance that he is from Africa, the Caribbean or Europe, and not the United States.

Black men in prison in America have become as American as apple pie. There are a lot of Black men in prisons and jails in the United States (about 1.1 million) than there are Black men incarcerated in the rest of the world combined. This criminalization process now starts in elementary schools with Black male children as young as six and seven years old being arrested in staggering numbers according to a 2005 report, Education on Lockdown by the Advancement Project.

The rest of the world is watching and following the lead of America. Other countries including England, Canada, Jamaica, Brazil and South Africa are adopting American social policies that encourage the incarceration and destruction of young Black men. This is leading to a world-wide catastrophe. But still, there is no adequate response from the American or global Black community.

Worst of all is the passivity, neglect and disengagement of the Black community concerning the future of our Black boys. We do little while the future lives of Black boys are being destroyed in record numbers. The schools that Black boys attend prepare them with skills that will make them obsolete before, and if, they graduate. In a strange and perverse way, the Black community, itself, has started to wage a kind of war against young Black men and has become part of this destructive process.

Who are young Black women going to marry? Who is going to build and maintain the economies of Black communities? Who is going to anchor strong families in the Black community? Who will young Black boys emulate as they grow into men? Where is the outrage of the Black community at the destruction of its Black boys? Where are the plans and the supportive actions to change this? Is this the beginning of the end of the Black people in America?

The list of those who have failed young Black men includes our government, our foundations, our schools, our media, our Black churches, our Black leaders, and even our parents. Ironically, experts say that the solutions to the problems of young Black men are simple and relatively inexpensive, but they may not be easy, practical or popular. It is not that we lack solutions as much as it is that we lack the will to implement these solutions to save Black boys. It seems that government is willing to pay billions of dollars to lock up young Black men, rather than the millions it would take to prepare them to become viable contributors and valued members of our society.

Please consider these simple goals that can lead to solutions for fixing the problems of young Black men:

Short term

1) Teach all Black boys to read at grade level by the third grade and to embrace education.
2) Provide positive role models for Black boys.
3) Create a stable home environment for Black boys that include contact with their fathers.
4) Ensure that Black boys have a strong spiritual base.
5) Control the negative media influences on Black boys.
6) Teach Black boys to respect all girls and women.

Long term

1) Invest as much money in educating Black boys as in locking up Black men.
2) Help connect Black boys to a positive vision of them in the future.
3) Create high expectations and help Black boys live to those high expectations.
4) Build a positive peer culture for Black boys.
5) Teach Black boys self-discipline, culture, and history.
6) Teach Black boys and the communities in which they live to embrace education and life-long learning.

More Facts

- 37.7% of Black men in the United States are not working (2006 Joint Economic Committee Study chaired by Senator Charles E. Schumer (D-NY)).
- 58% of Black boys in the United States do not graduate from high school (2006 Report from the Schott Foundation for Public Education).
- Almost 70% of Black children are born into female, single-parent households (2000 Census Report).
- About 1 million Black men in the United States are in prison (U.S. Justice Department).

Phillip Jackson

Executive Director of the Black Star Project

Chicago, Il. blackstar1000@ameritech.net

Bibliography

American Sociological Review, 2004, Vol. 69 (April: 151-169), Mass_ Imprisonment_and_the _life_Race_and_Class_Ineq [1].pdf

Andrews, Dale. Practical Theology for Black Churches: Bridging Black Theology and African American Folk Religion. Louisville: Westminster John Knox Press, 2002.

Antioch Agenda. Eds. Daniel Jeyaraj, Robert W. Pazmino, and Rodney L. Petersen. New Delhi: Indian Society for the Promotion of Christian Knowledge, 2007.

Booth, Edward. Saint Augustine and the Western Tradition of Self-Knowing. Philadelphia: Villanova University Press, 1989.

Bourke, Vernon J. The Essential Augustine. Indiana: Hackett Publishing Company 1974.

Bowne, Parker Borden. Theory of Thought and Knowledge. New York: Harper & Brothers Publishers, 1897.

Bowne, Parker, Borden. Personalism. Norwood MA: The Plimpton Press, 1908.

Brown, Peter. Augustine of Hippo. Los Angeles: University of California Press, 1967.

Brightman, Edgar S., Moral Laws (New York: The Abingdon Press, 1933) Brightman, Edgar S. Person and Reality. Ed. Peter A. Bertocci. New York: Ronald Press, 1958.

Brightman, Edgar S. The Spiritual Life. New York: Abingdon Press, 1942.

Brightman, E.S. Ed. Personalism in Theology: Essay in Honor of Albert C. Knudson. Boston: Boston University Press, 1943.

Burnell, Peter. The Augustinian Person. Washington, D.C.: The Catholic University of America Press, 2005.

Burrow, Rufus Jr. Personalism: A Critical Introduction. Missouri: Chalice Press, 1999.

Clark, Mary. Augustine of Hippo: Selected Writings. New York: Paulist Press, 1984.

Criminal Justice: Race and Criminal Justice, in Compact for Racial Justice: An Agenda for Fairness and United (A proactive plan for fairness and unity in our communities, politics, the economy and the law, Applied Research Center) rd_compact_final.pdf, 17

De Chardin, Pierre Teilhard. The Divine Milieu: An Essay on the Interior Life. New York: Harper & Row, 1957.

Dickey, Laurence, and H.B. Nisbet, Eds. Hegel, G. W. F. Political Writings. Cambridge: Cambridge University, 1999.

Douglas, Kelly Brown. What's Faith Got to Do with It? New York: Orbis Book, 2005.

Du Bois, W. E. B. Darkwater: Voice from Within the Veil. New York: Schocken Book, 1969.

Du Bois, W.E. B. The Souls of Black Folk. New York: Dover Publications, Inc. 1994

Foster, Charles. Black Religious Experience: Conversation on Double Consciousness and the work of Grant Shockley. Nashville: Abingdon, 2003.

Fr. Thomas McGovern, The Christian Anthropology of John Paul 11: An Overview (www.Christendom-awake.org/pages/mcgovern/chrisanthro. htm.)

Fux, Pierre-Yves. Augustinus Afer: Saint Augustin: africanité et universalité, Actes du colloque international Algers-Annaba, 17 avril 200. Suisse: Editions Universitaires Fribourg Suisse, 2003.

Harrison, Carol. Augustine: Christian Truth and Fractured Humanity. Oxford: Oxford University Press, 2000.

Hegel, G.W.F. Phenomenology of Spirit. Translated by A. V. Miller. New York: Oxford University Press, 1977.

Hegel, Georg Wilhelm Friedrich. Lectures on the Philosophy of World History. Translated by H.B. Nisbet. New York: Cambridge University Press, 1975.

Hegel, G.W.F. *Elements of the Philosophy of Right*. Translated by Allen W. Wood and H. B. Nisbet. Cambridge: Cambridge University Press, 1991.

Huntington, Samuel P. The Clash of Civilization and the Remaking of the World Order. New York: Simon & Schuster, 1997.

Jones, Whitney. Basic Writings of Saint Augustine. New York: Random House Publishers, 1948.

Johnson, Ben Campbell. *Rethinking Evangelism: A Theological Approach*. Philadelphia: The Westminster Press, 1987.

John Paul 11, The Task of the World Culture of Today Is to Promote the Civilization of Love (3 April 1987) no. 4, in English-language weekly edition of L'Osservatore Romano 4 May 1987.

Karberg, Jennifer C., and Beck, Allen J. "Trends in U.S. Correctional Populations: Findings from the Bureau of Justice Statistics." Presented at the National Committee on Community Corrections Meeting, Washington, DC, April 16, 2004.

Kehr, Marguerite Witmer. The Doctrine of the Self in St. Augustine and in

Descartes The Philosophical Review, Vol. 25, No. 4 (Jul. 1916), pp.587-615.

Kirkham, Donald Henry. "Pamphlet Opposition to the Rise of Methodism: The Eighteenth-Century English Evangelical Revival Under Attack," (PhD, diss., Duke University, 1973, p. 202) 21: 333

Lewis, David Levering. W.E.B. Du Bois: Biography of a Race 1868-1919, New York: Henry Holt and Company, 1993

Lewis, David Levering, W.E.B. Du Bois: The Fight for Equality and the American Century: 1919-1963. New York: Henry Holt and Company, 2000

Lubac, Henri de. Augustinianism and Modern Theology. New York: The Crossroad Publishing Company, 2000. Sociology of Religion pg. 241. 2002, 63: 2 239-253

Marshall, Christopher D. Beyond Retribution: A New Testament Vision for Justice, Crime and Punishment. Michigan: William B. Eerdmans Publishing Company 2001

Marshall, Christopher D. Prison, Prisoners and the Bible (A paper delivered to "Breaking Down the Walls Conference," Tukua Nga Here Kia Marama Ai, Matamata, 14-16 June 2002 [Accessed. Feb. 2, 2009)

Marc Mauer, Racial Impact Statements as a Means of Reducing Unwarranted Sentencing Disparities, rd_racialimpactstatements.p df, 22, Accessed01/31/09.

Fr. Thomas McGovern. The Christian Anthropology of John Paul 11: An Overview www.Christendom-awake.org/pages/mcgovern/ chrisanthro.htm

Vatican Council 11, Gaudium et Spes (GS) (The Church in the Modern World, 1965) and Dignitatis Humanae (Decree on Religious Freedom, 1965). 22.

Meagher, Robert E. An Introduction to Augustine. New York, New York University Press, 1978.

Nash, Ronald H. The light of the mind: St. Augustine's Theory of Knowledge. Kentucky: The University Press of Kentucky, 1969.

Neuhouser, Frederick. Foundation of Hegel's Social Theory: Actualizing Freedom. London: Harvard University Press, 2000.

O'Connell, Robert J. St. Augustine's Early Theory of Man, AD 386-391.Massachusetts: The Belknap Press of Harvard University Press, 1968.

Portalie, Eugene. A Guide to The Thought of Saint Augustine. Chicago: Henry Regnery Company 1960)

Rawls, John. The Law of Peoples: with "The Idea of Public Reason Revisited. London, Harvard University Press, 2002.

Rawls, John. Justice as Fairness: A Restatement. New Delhi, Universal, Low Publishing Co. Pvt. Ltd. 2001.

Rawls, John. Political Liberalism (New York, Columbia University Press, 2005),

Rizer, Arthur L. 111, The Race Effect on Wrongful Convictions: Rizer Article formatted Current. Doc, 7_Rizer [1].pdf, William Mitchell Law Review, Vol. 29:3 p 848. (Susan H. Bitensky, Section 1983: Agent of Peace or Vehicle of Violence Against Children, 54 OKLA. L. Rev. 333, 372 n.61 (2001);

Constance R. LeSage, The Death Penalty for Rape-Cruel and Unusual Punishment? 38 LA. L. Rev. 868, 870 n.8 (1978).

Russell, Robert P. Saint Augustine and the Augustinian Tradition. Philadelphia: Villanova University Press, 1970.

Saint Augustine: Confessions. Trans. Henry Chadwick, Oxford: Oxford University Press, 1991.

Saint Augustine: The City of God. Trans. Marcus Dods, New York: The Modern Library, 1993.

Saint Augustine: The Trinity. (De Trinitate) A.D. 400-416; PL 42, 8191098; trans. Marcus Dods, vol. V11.

Saint Augustine: The Teacher (De Magistro) A.D. 389; PL, 32, 1193-1220; trans. G. C. Leckie.

Saint Augustine: Soliloquies, 11 (Soliloquia) AD 387; PL 32, 869-904; trans. Nicene, vol. V11 (1888); Marcus Dods, reprinted in Oates, 1,259-297; FOC 5 (1948); LCC 6 (1953). (

Saint Augustine: Answers to Seven Questions for Simplicianus, (De diversis quaestionibus V11 ad Simplicianum) AD 396-367; PL 40, 101-148; LCC 6 (1953), trans. V. J. Bourke

Saint Augustine: On Music, V1. 5: 12-13 (De Música) AD 387-391; PL32, 1081-1194; trans. FOC 4 (1947); Bk. V1 only, T. P. Mahar, S. J., St. Louis U. Thesis, 1939.

Saint Augustine: On the True Religio., (De vera religione) AD 389-391; PL 34, 121-172; trans C.A. Hangartner, S.J., De vera religione (Chapters1-17) St. Louis University Master's Thesis, 1945.

Stock, Brian. After Augustine: The Meditative Reader and the Text. Philadelphia: University of Pennsylvania Press, 2001.

Stone, Ronald. John Wesley's Life & Ethics. Nashville: Abingdon Press2001)

Sundquist, Eric, J. Ed., W.E.B. Du Bois Reader. Oxford: Oxford University Press, 1996.

The Covenant with Black America. Chicago: Third World Press, 2006.

The Methodist Review 1897 (http://docsouth.unc.edu/chu rch/bowen/bio.html)

Thomas Jefferson, "Notes on the State of Virginia," in The Life and Selected Writings of Thomas Jefferson, ed. Adrienne Koch and William Peden. New York: Modern Library, 1998.

Tillich, Paul. Systematic Theology. Vol. one. London: The University of Chicago Press, 1951.

Thurman, Howard. With Head and Heart: The Autobiography of Howard Thurman. New York: Harcourt Brace & Company, 1979.

Vatican Council 11. Gaudium et Spes (GS) (The Church in the Modern World, 1965) and Dignitatis Humanae (Decree on Religious Freedom, 1965).

Wesley, John. The Works of John Wesley. Ed. Richard P. Heitzenrater, The Bicentennial Edition, vol. 21.

Nashville, Tennessee: Abingdon Press, 1992.

Wesley, John. The Works of John Wesley. Richard P. Heitzenrater, The Bicentennial Edition, vol. 19. Nashville, Tennessee: Abingdon Press, 1990

Wesley, John. The Works of John Wesley. Richard P. Heitzenrater, The Bicentennial Edition, vol. 20. Nashville, Tennessee: Abingdon Press, 1991.

West, Cornel, Race Matters. New York: Vintage Books, 2001.

Wilmore, Gayraud S. Black Religion, and Black Radicalism: An Interpretation of the Religious History of Afro-American People. New York: Orbis Books, 1994.

Wittgenstein, Ludwig. Blue and Brown Books. USA: Harper and Row Publishers, 1958

Wogaman, J. Philip (Ed). Communitarian Ethics: Later

Writings of Walter G. Muelder. (Maine: The Preachers' Aid Society of New England in cooperation with BW press, 2007.

Zuckerman, Phil. Ed. The Social Theory of W.E.B. Du Bois. California: Pine Forge Press, 2004.

Lockwood, Daniel. Prison Sexual Violence, Elsevier, New York, 1980 From Christ to the World: Introductory Readings in Christian Ethics, Eds. Wayne G. Boulton, Thomas D. Kennedy, Allen Verhey (Grand Rapids, Michigan, William B. Eerdmans Publishing Company,1994)

Reiman, Jeffrey The Rich Get Richer, and the Poor Get Prison: Ideology, Class, and Criminal Justice (New York, John Wiley & Sons 1984) Pp. 1.

Shichor, David, Punishment for Profit: Private Prisons/Public Concerns (London, Sage Publications, 1995)

Ives, George. A History of Penal Methods: Criminals, Witches, Lunatics, p, 366.

Elikann, Peter T. The Tough-On-Crime Myth: Real Solution to Cut Crime, (Insight Books, Planum Press, New York and London, 1996),

Economic Justice for All: Pastoral Letter on Catholic Social Teaching and the U.S. Economy (Washington, D.C: U.S. Catholic Conference, 1986, Pp. 15.

Carroll, James "Is It Time to Dismantle the Revenge Machine?" Boston Globe3 (February 8, 1994)

Business Wire: New Federal Report: Sexual Abuse Plagues U.S. Prisons and Jails, 2010 (http://www.businesswire.com/news/home/20100826005772/en/Federal,

Insideprison.com, Prison Rape: The Challenge of Prevention and Enforcement, 2006,

(http://www.insideprison.co
m/prison-rape.asp,)

Jeff Seidel, MI: Sexual
Abuse of Women Went
Unheeded-2 of 5 articles and
Human Rights Watch
Report. 2009.
(http://realcostofprisons.org/
blog/archives/2009/01/mi_a
b

Nicole Summer, Powerless
in Prison: Sexual Abuse
Against Incarcerated
Women, 2007,
(http://www.rhrealitycheck.o
rg/print/5597.

Christopher Hitchens, The
Scandalous Brutality of U.S.
Prisons. In VanityFair, 2005
(http://www.vanityfair.com/
politics/features/2005/09hitc
hens200,

National Women's Law
Center, (The Rebecca Project
for Human Rights) 2010,
Mothers Behind Bars: A
State-by-state report card and
analysis of federal policies
on conditions of confinement
for pregnant and parenting
women and the effect on their
children.

Human Rights Watch:
http://www.hrw.org/reports/
2001/prison/ report.html

settings"(http://beyond-the-
illusion.
com/files/issues/condom.txt)
.

Shelley Murphy, MA:
Another Suicide Raises
Questions About Safety of
MA Prisoners, August 16th
2010, the Boston Globe
(http://realcostofprisons.org/b
log/archives/2010/08/ma_ano
ther_s)

Criminal Justice,
(http://criminaljustice.change.
org/blog/view/why_massasac
husetts_h)

http://realcostofprisons.org/bl
og/archives/2009/01/va_deat
h_in

Lendman, Stephen, Torture
in US Prisons, 2010,
(http://www.rense.com/gene
ral92/TORTURE.HTM

Bureau of Justice Statistics:
Special Report: Sexual
Victimization in Juvenile
Facilities Reported by Youth,

2008-2009,
http://bjs.ojp.usdoj.gov/cont
ent/pub/pdf/svjfry09.pdf

Vincent Schiraldi and
Mariam M. Bell: Prison Rape
Is No Joke, The Washington
Post, June 13[th,] 2002,
(http://www.vachss.com/hel
p_text/archive/no_joke.html)

Michel Martin, Sexual Abuse
Persists in Juvenile Detention
Centers, 2010,
(http://www.npr.org/template
s/story/story.php/storyld=127
536419

Buchanan, Kim Shayo,
Impunity: Sexual Abuse in
Women's Prisons, 2007, Pp.
47, (Harvard Civil Rights-
Civil Liberties Law Review,
Vol. 42)

Brendan Kirby, Blacks 4
Times More Likely to End
Up in Juvenile System,
(http://blog.al.com/live//print
.html

Minority Disproportionality
Exists at Various; Decisions
Points in the Juvenile Justice
System.

(http://www.ncjrs.gov/html/
ojjdp/202885/page11.html

W. Haywood Burns Institute:
Adoration of the Question:
Reflections on the Failure to
Reduce Racial & Ethnic
Disparities in the Juvenile
Justice System:
http://www.burnsinstitute.or
g/downloads/BI%20Adorati
on%20of%20the%20Questio
n.pdf
www.familiesoffreedom.org
April 2, 2008
http://.www.Therealcostofpri
son.com
http://jjpl.org/new/
http://bjs.ojp.usdoj.gov/cont
ent/pub/pdf/svjfry09.pdf
http://docsouth.unc.edu/chur
ch/bowen/bio.html
http://www.duboisle.org/htm
l/DuBoisBio.html
www.sentencingproject.org/
pdfs/brownboard.pdf, the
Sentencing Project.")
http://www.ojp.usdoj.gov/bj
s/pub/pdf/wo.pdf.
(http://gbgm-
umc.org/mission_programs/
mcr/4.35/theprison.cfm
http://www.hrw.org/reports/
2001/prison/report.html
http://www.ussc.gov/crack/e
xecsum.pdf

http://www.sentencingprojec
t.org
http://www.heritage.org
http://www.sentencingproject.
org/NewsDetails.aspx?NewsI
D=454
http://www.sentencingproject.
org/NewsDetails.aspx?NewsI
D=454
www.Sentencingproject.org/
rd_brownvboard[1].pdf

www.Sentencingproject.org/
rd_brownvboard[1].pdf

www.Sentencingproject.org/
rd_brownvboard[1].pdf

www.Sentencingproject.org/
rd_brownvboard[1].pdf
www.Sentencingproject.org/
rd_brownvboard[1].pdf
rd_crisisoftheyoung [1].pdf
http://www.latimes.com/new
s/local/la-me-nolan5ju105,
http://www.hrw.org/reports/
2000/usa/Rcedrg00-01.htm
www.Sentencingproject.org/
rd_brownvboard[1].pdf,
www.Sentencingproject.org/
rd_brownvboard[1].pdf,
http://www.abcnews.go.com
/pringt?

http://www.beyond-the-
illusion.com/files/issues/con
dom.txt
http://www.seattlepi.nwsour
ce.com/local/300173_prison
18.html

www.washingtonpost.com/w
p-
dyn/content/story/02/28/ST2
008022803016.html.[299]